THE Enduring *Library*

TECHNOLOGY, TRADITION, AND THE QUEST FOR BALANCE

Michael Gorman

AMERICAN LIBRA[RY]
Chicago

D1166323

Portions of this book appeared in a different form in *Library Journal, Information Technology and Libraries, Library Trends,* and the *IFLA Journal.*

While extensive effort has gone into ensuring the reliability of information appearing in this book, the publisher makes no warranty, express or implied, on the accuracy or reliability of the information, and does not assume and hereby disclaims any liability to any person for any loss or damage caused by errors or omissions in this publication.

Design and composition by ALA Editions in Berkeley Book, Alexa, and Futura Condensed using QuarkXPress 4.1 on a PC platform

Printed on 50-pound white offset and bound in 10-point coated cover stock by McNaughton & Gunn

The paper used in this publication meets the minimum requirements of American National Standard for Information Sciences—Permanence of Paper for Printed Library Materials, ANSI Z39.48-1992. ∞

Library of Congress Cataloging-in-Publication Data

Gorman, Michael, 1941–
    The enduring library : technology, tradition, and the quest for balance / by Michael Gorman.
        p.   cm.
    ISBN 0-8389-0846-2
    1. Libraries and society. 2. Libraries—Aims and objectives. 3. Libraries—Automation. 4. Library science—Technological innovations. 5. Library science—Forecasting. 6. Librarians—Professional ethics. I. Title.
    Z716.4.G665 2003
    021.2—dc21   2002151679

Printed in the United States of America

07   06   05   04   03   5   4   3   2   1

This book is dedicated to

LOUIS DEXTER GORMAN
and
BESS ROSA GORMAN

CONTENTS

ACKNOWLEDGMENTS   vii

INTRODUCTION   ix

Libraries and Communications Technology

1   The Way We Live Now: Libraries Today   1
2   Communications Technology, 1875 to Now   14
3   Communications Technology and Libraries Today   27

Reading and the Web

4   Reading in a Digital World   40
5   The Nature of the Web   52

Library Work and the Future of Libraries

6   Reference Work in Technologically Advanced Libraries   66
7   Cataloguing in the Twenty-First Century   82
8   Challenges of the Future   95
9   The Future of Libraries: A Research Agenda   110

Overcoming Stress and Achieving Harmony

10 Information Overload and Stress: The Ailments
of Modern Living   122

11 Seeking Harmony and Balance   134

INDEX   149

ACKNOWLEDGMENTS

I wish to acknowledge the help of a number of my colleagues in the Madden Library at Fresno State for their witting or unwitting contributions to this book. In particular, I would like to thank Dave Tyckoson, Ross LaBaugh, Patrick Newell, Karen Kinney, Angelica Carpenter, and Pat Lavigna. My provost, Michael Ortiz, could not possibly be more supportive or encouraging. I am also grateful to my colleagues and friends in other places: Anne Heanue, Wilma Minty, Anne Reuland, Sherrie Schmidt, John Byrum, Michael Buckland, and Kerrie Talmacs. I discussed one chapter of this book with the late and much missed Brett Butler and profited from his insights. I thank my assistants Susan Mangini and Bernie Griffith for their infinite patience and ever-present resourcefulness. The editors at ALA Editions, especially Marlene Chamberlain, Mary Huchting, and Paul Mendelson, have been patient, persevering, and immensely helpful.

As ever, I am more grateful than I can say for the love of my daughters Emma Celeste Gorman and Alice Clara Gorman. They are the light of my life.

INTRODUCTION

*In times of change and danger, when there is a quicksand of fear
under men's reasoning, a sense of continuity with generations
gone before can stretch like a lifeline across the scary present.*

—John Dos Passos[1]

George Eliot's *Middlemarch,* deemed by many the finest English-language novel of the nineteenth century, is rooted in a particular time and place. The time is the late 1820s and early 1830s and the place England—a country going through a profound change. Superstition was giving way to science, quackery to scientific medicine, stagecoaches to railroads, cottage industries and hand implements to factories and machinery, and the nation was still consumed with the controversies attendant on the First Reform Bill, finally enacted in 1832. The changes and societal shifts seemed epochal and transformational to the people of the time about which Eliot was writing (forty years later)—as indeed they were. The novel would lack much of its resonance if it were set in quieter, more settled times. The rub is, of course, to find any such times. The American and French Revolutions had taken place a scant fifty years before the events of *Middlemarch*—and they were epochal, the best of times and the worst of times. The European revolutions of 1848 lay between the times in which *Middlemarch* is set and the writing of the book, and they were seen as transforming the Continent. The First World War broke out thirty-four years after George Eliot died. It was called "the war to end all wars" and is seen by many as the defining line between the Victorian age and modern times. I could go on with a familiar litany of political, military, and social defining moments—the "quiet bland" Eisenhower 1950s were, after all, the time of the "red scare," the stirrings of the civil rights movement, and the very real fears of nuclear war that still haunt most who were children then. At the time of writing the United States and the world are still reeling from the awful events of September 11, 2001—"a day in which the whole world changed," we are told constantly.

These are all great events for good or ill and I wish in no way to belittle their importance, but merely to point out that each age has its clashes between the past and the present, its fears of current calamities and unknown future changes. I have concentrated on the political and military, but one could make exactly the same point about technology. Most now feel only nostalgia for the rural railroads, but the characters in *Middlemarch* feared and resisted what they saw as a "monstrous intrusion into the countryside that might be repulsed."[2] The events in *Middlemarch* take place not long after the Luddites had smashed the weaving machines in an ultimately futile gesture against what they saw, quite correctly, as a threat to their livelihoods, to their way of life, and to rural society as a whole. Now here we are, at the end of two centuries that have brought us transformational technologies from the steam engine to the computer, thinking, as people in all ages do, that we have reached some unsurpassable level of technological achievement and are on the threshold of an entirely new age. To a certain extent, that last is true and will remain true until the next transformational technology ushers in yet another "unique" period of change. I think the belief that one's own time is unique is a hindrance to clear thinking and makes it very difficult, in libraries and elsewhere, to make rational and cost-effective judgments about how best to use limited human and financial resources.

I seek in this book to describe our present and future library life, our use of technology, and our ways of looking at what we do. I also seek to describe a balanced approach that will enable us to incorporate technology (especially digital technology) harmoniously and without compromising our basic values. The technology that concerns us most is that which relates to communication—the conveying of messages. This has always been the case, since libraries have always dealt, and still deal, with recorded knowledge and information—with complex messages between the dead and the living, the living and the living, and the living and people as yet unborn—irrespective of the technology used to make those records available and to preserve them for future generations.

Humankind has been making such records for ten millennia—we know this because one of the technologies used then (impressions on clay tablets) proved to be durable across those millennia.[3] Another early technology—ink on papyrus and, later, prepared animal skin—was more perishable, but some examples and fragments have survived, to give us at least an idea of what the earliest recorded knowledge and information was like. Millennia later, the scroll and the codex became the dominant communication technologies, the latter triumphing after the Western invention of printing in the fifteenth century. In the last 150 years, the written and printed word have coexisted with a variety of other means of recording texts, sounds, and images. A dizzying array of such means—from nineteenth-century sound recordings on wire to twenty-first-century CDs; microforms of many kinds; film, videos, DVDs; multimedia productions; and, of course, digital electronic documents and resources—has influenced the way we live and communicate. Since all these technologies are the very stuff of what libraries are about, each has had a great impact on the nature and functioning of libraries.

It is a feature of society as a whole and libraries in particular that the newest technology is always received with irrational ardor and is always seen as transformational. In just the last sixty-five years, radio has been proclaimed the answer to universal higher education, television the death of the movie industry, microforms the ultimate solution to library space problems, audiovisual materials the cause of changing libraries into "resource centers," and the "virtual library" and the "information superhighway" have been proclaimed the answers to all that ails society. If you look at each of these examples, you will see a predictable series of stages.

Incomprehension. Few know about or understand the technology.

Underestimation. Most deride the few enthusiasts that proclaim the technology transformational.

Acceptance. The technology becomes widely understood and used.

Overestimation. Great claims are made for the effect of the technology and those claims are widely accepted. At the same time we see . . .

Resistance. A minority sees the dark side of the technology as a menace to civilization and standards.

Incorporation. Inappropriate or inefficient applications of the technology wither on the vine. The technology is prized for what it does well and accepted as a part of normal life while we wait for . . .

New technology. Something new is invented that starts the cycle all over again.

Of the seven stages listed above, we have been through or are living in the first five and can see the last two peeking around the corner. What is past is prologue, and the computer will take its place with all the other communications technologies in our lives and our libraries as we learn to prize it for what it can do well and rely on other technologies for what it cannot do well. It is all a question of balance and seeking harmony and understanding. This book is, in part, about the effect of computer technology on libraries, but it is also about the questions raised by the use of that technology and advocates achieving a new librarianship that combines our history with modernity in service to our users, society, and posterity.

How can communications technology enhance our work and our lives without degrading either? What is the best way to advance and preserve the human record? What does it mean to be literate and to advance literacy in a society that seems, in many ways, postliterate? How can we balance the ability to communicate and the need for reflection in a hurried, harried world? These and many other questions dog our minds and form the conscious or unconscious subtext of our library lives. Some of these questions are universal. Some apply, or should apply, to all those living and working in developed countries in the early twenty-first century. Others are peculiar to librarians.

I begin this book with a look at where libraries stand today and their opportunities and perils. This is followed by a survey of communications technology from the 1870s to the recent past, and by a portrait of that technology today and the immediate future. I follow these with a chapter on literacy and reading in a digital world. I then examine that modern phenomenon—the World Wide Web—from the point of view of providing a taxonomy aimed at identifying its worthwhile elements. Collection development, reference work, and cataloguing (under whichever names you choose) are the pillars of librarianship. I examine them in the light of our present circumstances. This discussion is followed by chapters on the challenges of the future and a research agenda for the future of libraries. Information overload and its concomitant stress are barriers to the acquisition of knowledge and learning. I close the book with my ideas on these modern afflictions and their cure through seeking harmony and balance.

Here is a true story that is also a fable for our times. The hype about the Internet and the illusion of fabulous wealth to be made with little or no effort reached its apogee in 1999. Billionaires, made so by doing nothing but selling their ideas to gullible venture capitalists and their stock to even more gullible investors, were riding high. The "new economy," that South Sea Bubble of our time, was said to have repealed the business cycle and brought us to a postcapitalist nirvana. In San Francisco, one of the epicenters of this hysteria, low-rent areas were invaded by black-clad dot.commers paying astronomical sums for space in which to spin their dreams into gold. One of the most popular areas for these elements was the distinctly down-market, but central, South of Market neighborhood. Artists, small businesses, and the like were driven from their lofts to seek dot.com-free areas. Among the victims was the Arion Press—one of the longest-lived and most venerated fine presses and type foundries in the city.

In the words of a *Los Angeles Times* article, the press "scrambled to find a new home for tons of historic equipment, monotype machines and letterpresses, a type foundry, a book bindery, and one of the most extensive collections of type fonts surviving today—which alone weighs 40 tons."[4] The press was being evicted to provide more room for Driveway.com ("an Internet provider of data storage"). The Arion Press is now housed in the Presidio (a former army base, now a national park in one of the most desirable areas of the city) and is finishing work on a limited-edition pulpit Bible, printed from type created on the premises and hand bound in the press's bindery. Its former South of Market location stands empty. Driveway.com, like hundreds of its ilk, has closed down. This begs the question: why does a technology that would be instantly recognizable to Johannes Gutenberg (1398–1468) survive and thrive when the dot.com revolution has died without ever really living? Why, in an age when a desktop computer gives access to many typographic fonts and technology has made the production of good-quality books more widespread, do letterpress printers continue to flourish? These are puzzling questions for a supposedly utilitarian age, and are worth pondering by all those with an interest in the ways in which humankind communicates and preserves its records. One thing we do know. Today's products of the Arion Press will be as readable and useful in 500 years as they are now, unless the world ends in fire and ice before then.

There is a fundamental premise behind this book. It is that, in order to understand the impact of technology on society and libraries, we need to have a clear view of the history and evolution of communications technology. In particular, we need to understand that there have been periods of history in which technology had a transformational impact that was at least comparable to our situation today. We must understand the past, our place in relation to that past, and the lessons it can teach us if we are to deal with the present rationally and face the future without fear.

NOTES

1. John Dos Passos, "The Use of the Past," in *The Ground We Stand On: Some Examples from the History of a Political Creed* (New York: Harcourt, Brace, 1941), 3. This essay was originally published in two parts as "Inspiration of Our History" in *The American Mercury* (August–September 1941).

2. Karen Chase, introduction to *Middlemarch,* by George Eliot (Cambridge: Cambridge University Press, 1991), 20. I am also grateful to Professor Chase for her insights into the context of *Middlemarch.*

3. James Westfall Thompson, *Ancient Libraries* (Berkeley: University of California Press, 1940).

4. Maria L. La Ganga, "There's No Stopping Those Letterpresses," *Los Angeles Times,* Tuesday, July 17, 2001, sec. B, pp. B1 and B8.

My approach is based on the Copernican principle, which has been one of the most famous and successful scientific hypotheses in the history of science. It's named after Nicolaus Copernicus, who proved that the earth is not the center of the universe; and it's simply the idea that your location is not special. The more we learn about the universe, the more non-special our location has looked. The earth is orbiting an ordinary star in an ordinary galaxy. The reason the Copernican principle works is that, of all the places for intelligent observers to be, there are by definition only a few special places and many non-special places. So, you are simply more likely to be in one of the many non-special places.

—J. Richard Gott III, as quoted by Timothy Ferris in
"How to Predict Everything," *New Yorker,* July 12, 1999, 35–39

1 The Way We Live Now
Libraries Today

H. F. LYTE'S ANGLICAN HYMN "ABIDE WITH ME," AFTER OBSERVING "FAST FALLS THE eventide," contains the famous line "Change and decay in all around I see." A more famous and modern composer—Bob Dylan—tells us "it's not dark yet, but it's getting there." Such darkling thoughts are tempting to those of us who are of a certain age and approaching retirement, but I think they should be resisted. I am sure that librarians in the later years of the Roman Empire thought that everything they had achieved was going to the proverbial destination in a handbasket, but they had the Dark Ages looming over them and can be forgiven a pessimistic slant. The humanist author A. C. Grayling has written:

> Every age thinks it is in crisis. Things have got worse, people say, clicking their tongues; crime is up, the quality of life down, the world is in a mess. People of a religious bent are inclined to think that their personal epoch is so bad that it probably marks the end of the world.
>
> Such sentiments are misleading because they promise a belief that somewhere or sometime the world had something that has since been lost—a cosy, chintzy afternoon-teatime era when there was neither danger without or unease within.[1]

WHAT AFFLICTS US ALL

Let us look at the problems that face all libraries to a greater or lesser extent:

The flight of library users from print sources because of the notion that "everything is available on the Web"

Funding for "traditional" materials and programs falling prey to funding for electronic resources and services at a time when there is no diminution of "traditional" publishing

Library administrations in thrall to notions of digital libraries and the like and out of touch with the pressures of frontline library work and the real needs of patrons

Public and school libraries having to take on more expansive but unfunded roles, particularly with regard to children

Pressure on academic and public libraries to incorporate, maintain, and pay for digital collections, databases, etc., many of them duplicative, and built up elsewhere in the community

Reluctance on the part of many administrators and boards of trustees to fund new and improved library buildings

Newly graduated librarians lacking an education in such basic library skills as reference service, cataloguing, etc.

The graying of the library profession, leading to the retirement of large numbers of librarians with irreplaceable skills

Libraries' increasing and unfunded participation in networks and other cooperative programs while seeking to meet the needs of the communities for which those libraries are funded

Greatly increased needs for library instruction and information-competence programs

The collapse of much of library education in the face of the assault of "information science" and the trend to digitization

A crisis in preservation—especially of digital electronic materials

We could all add to this list of pressures and woes and could be forgiven for pessimism or even the sin of despair. There are two reasons why I at least believe such reactions are unwarranted. The first is that all of us, in every age, suffer from the disease of thinking that our time and our predicament are unique and that change is uniquely transformational. The Copernican principle advanced by J. Richard Gott tells us that just as the Earth is not a special place, galactically speaking, any given time is also likely to be unexceptional. We see our home planet as special because it is all we have. Similarly, we tend to see our own era as special because it is the only one we have in which to live.

The second reason for being positive follows from the first. If this is not an exceptional time, why should we assume that it will differ from all other such times in the history of human communication and the history of libraries? It is more logical to assume that we are merely at a given point in the steady evolution of libraries and human communication, with much change behind us and much change yet to come. Given that understanding, we as a profession can relax and deal with our problems coolly and on the basis of analysis and logic—evolutionary times call for evolutionary responses. The chief evolutionary response is, of course, the incorporation of computer technology and digital communication into library services in a balanced and practical way. To take the opposite view is to proclaim a revolution calling for nothing less than the overthrow of all existing structures. In the case of libraries, this would mean the end of the library as a physical place, the redefinition of the profession of librarianship, the substitution of information services for collections of recorded knowledge, and the abandonment of traditional library services and programs (reference service, bibliographic control, and so on). This is what lies behind all the discussion about "paradigm shifts," "reengineering," and the other tattered remnants of now-discredited management theories. How much more logical it is to take a humane, evolutionary point of view, to work on both innovation and preservation, and to advance the commitment to learning and civilization that has characterized the history of libraries.

THE DIVERSITY OF LIBRARIES

There is a golden thread of values and practices that runs through library work in all kinds of libraries—a golden thread that defines librarianship as a profession no matter where it is practiced. However, one has to acknowledge the enormous diversity of libraries. They vary in their size, mission, location, funding sources, staffing, and, these days, in the proportion of their budgets spent on computer technology. There is a vast difference between, say, the small library of a private law practice and the library of a major public research university; although they are both libraries, there are more characteristics that separate than unite them. Each of them, in turn, is very different from the library of a large suburban school district and a rural branch public library. Despite our libraries' diversity, it is important to understand that the Library of Congress (LC) shares a mutuality of mission with a mobile library on the road in the wilds of Idaho. They are both about making the records of humanity available to their users and providing ancillary services to assist toward that end. The specialist librarians at the LC are about the same work as the person staffing that mobile library—serving the scholars and dilettantes using the former and the adults and children looking forward to the arrival of the latter.

Libraries, as with other human institutions, have choices, and often a complex and multidimensional mesh of choices. The results are both beneficial and dark. For every libraryless "university" that advertises expensive degrees with a minimum of effort and a maximum of fees, there is a real university with a real library featured prominently in its fund-raising brochures. However, that same university is probably heavily invested in "distance learning" projects whose students have access only to electronic databases and preset packages of readings. The underlying, implicit message is that you can get a quality higher education without access to a real academic library. Both academic and public libraries devote increasing portions of their budgets to the provision of computer terminals and the databases to which they give access. Well-financed K–12 schools—usually in the suburban penumbra of big cities, but also encountered in small towns that house universities or high-tech industries—have excellent, comprehensive libraries with both current books and a technological infrastructure. Poorly financed K–12 schools are likely to have libraries with neither, when they have libraries at all. The Gates Foundation has a major program to wire school and public libraries in "disadvantaged" (poor) areas, but not, to my knowledge, a parallel program to supply those libraries with the books and librarians they desperately lack. The digital divide is a somber reality for large minorities of the population, but the library and literacy divides are even more expansive, darker, and far less easily remedied.

LIBRARY BUILDINGS: SYMBOLS AND MANIFESTATIONS

True, the library isn't sexy or fashionable. It isn't a place
to see or be seen. But in times when nothing is certain,
it gives me endless comfort and pleasure.[2]

Libraries lead a strange life in the popular imagination. For every newspaper and magazine article about the supremacy of the Internet and young people living in an entirely digital world, there is a contrary article about the importance of books and reading and the value of "the library" (usually a public library building is implied) to neighborhoods and to society. Both types of article almost invariably get it wrong—or to be more charitable, depend on myths and stereotypes for their sustenance. For example, magazines and newspapers chronicle the threats to local library service and older library buildings and the complex battles waged over them without seeming to grasp that library buildings are both symbols and manifestations. They are symbols of learning and of their communities' commitment to learning, but they are also those aspirations made manifest. A discussion about the rebirth or replacement of an old library building takes place at both the symbolic and the practical level. What does the community want the library building to be, but also what does the community want the library building to stand for? An English journalist wrote:

> Bitter battles are being waged over the future of the public library. Cambridge, Leicester, Stoke-on-Trent and the east London borough of Tower Hamlets are just some of the places where traditionalists—more often than not educated, white and middle class—are pitted against modernising councillors and local authority staff who argue that closing older, under-used libraries and relocating to new, hi-tech buildings in shopping centres will attract people who fail to use the service.[3]

Note that class, education, and age are taken to be factors in such discussions and that two seemingly opposing tendencies in society are pitted against each other over a vision of society as much as the location and nature of particular buildings. Similar clashes are replicated all over the Western world as the idea of the library as a center of the intellectual and educational life of the community is thought to be giving way to something that is seen as having lesser importance—the library as "information center," offering a service of no greater importance than any other. (I should probably note here that when I refer to "community," I am using the word in a broad sense—the community can be a municipality, metropolis, academic institution, school, company, research center, government agency, or any other gathering of people around a place or mission.) The debate is always, at bottom, about the role of the library in that community or, indeed, whether that community needs anything recognizable as a library. Such disputes are generally seen as being between modernizers and "small c" conservatives and may in many instances be so. As with most human interactions, however, such debates have many layers and nuances. The choice is not between ancient and modern, technology and books, spirituality and materialism, learning and entertainment, information and knowledge, or any of the other dichotomies that bedevil us. It is, rather, about how to balance these factors and create something that has the best of each. Libraries are complex organisms that have shown a remarkable capacity over the years to adapt and adopt, to change while hewing to enduring values. The buildings that house and, to a certain extent, define libraries are both manifestations and symbols of these clashes and choices. Some members of a community revere old library buildings that, to them, stand for the values of the past. Others are neophiliac—

admiring the new because it is new. Yet others (probably the majority) appreciate both the grandeur of the old and the efficiency and other pleasures of the new. All three can come together in the renovation of a library building—a magnificent example of which is the main building of the New York Public Library.

An architect and a librarian have advanced nine factors that affect the design and construction of new academic libraries.[4] These factors can stand for all library buildings (I have added my gloss in italics, when necessary, to their list) and lie at the heart of success or failure in marrying the new with the old.

The growing importance of electronics *or, possibly, the perceived need for ever more digitized resources*

The shift from exclusively individual learning to individual and collaborative learning. *This is a fashionable notion in academia and may be no more than the spotlight falling on something that has been going on for decades— but the modern library of any kind must provide areas in which two or more library users may engage in projects together.*

Community and institutional pride

The emerging role of libraries as campus centers and information commons. *This too, especially the latter phrase, is trendiness masking an eternal reality. The library has always been a "center," a place to foregather, and a resource for communities within communities. A good library building will recognize this fact.*

The need for less expensive ways to store print *(and all tangible collections)*

The importance of historical materials *(archives, special collections, and the like)*

Differing concepts about staff-staff and staff-user relationships. *The type of physical space for library workers and for person-to-person services differs from library to library and there can be no standard answer, even for two very similar libraries of the same type.*

Uncertainty about the future

Site, budget, and design considerations

Any library that employs these nine factors wisely will produce a building (money permitting) that expresses the aspirations and history of the community and supports the full range of services and programs that community needs.

We must be clear in considering library buildings and look beyond the outward signs of one stance or another. For instance, calling a new college library an "Information Center" is silly, but it is not a capital offense. That library may actually be both functional and beautiful and its name matters very little in the scheme of things. The impressive Lied Library at the University of Nevada, Las Vegas (opened in 2001), includes a café and positively encourages the consumption of food and drink in the library. Some might find this unduly permissive and worry about the wear and tear on books, carpets, and furniture, but it is scarcely a fatal flaw in a major modern library building, not least because library users consume food and drinks in libraries anyway—even in those in which comestibles are banned. It may seem odd for a public library to close a neighborhood branch and move it to a shopping mall, but that may be both an acceptance of reality and a view of the mall as the twenty-first-century town square. On the other hand, older people without cars and children for whom the mall is an occasional family treat may well have used the closed neighborhood branch disproportionately and frequently. The dilemma lies in the choice between a larger potential clientele and the actual needs of those for whom the neighborhood library may be the most important social amenity.

The library is both symbolized and made manifest in the space and structures it occupies. It also transcends that space and structure—especially today when technology extends the reach of the library to much greater distances than ever before. Anyone using the wonderful America's Story website is as much a user of the Library of Congress as a person sitting in the Main Reading Room of the Jefferson Building on 1st Street, SE, in Washington, D.C.[5] That remote use is made possible by means of computer technology, specifically the World Wide Web. However, a means (communication) to an end is useless without content. In a fundamental sense it is wrong to say that the Web makes the America's Story site possible. America's Story already exists in the enormous collections held in the Library of Congress's Madison, Jefferson, and Adams buildings and other storage spaces. It is the content held in archives and libraries that constitutes the human record, not the means that delivers that content. Technology can extend the programs and services of the LC and any other library, but the library's collections are the essence of such services. The vast majority of worthwhile documents and resources in the human record are in print and other nondigital forms or are simultaneously in nondigital *and* digital forms. There is a sliver of material of enduring value of that record, of unknown dimensions, that exists digitally and only digitally. This is the most endangered part of the human record since Gutenberg brought print to the Western world. As such, it deserves attention. That attention should not be all consuming, nor should the value of technology as a conduit blind us to the transcendent value of the content disseminated via that conduit.

OUR COLLECTIONS

This brings us to the knotty question of what constitutes a library collection in the modern world. It has been more than a century since that question could be answered simply in terms of physical objects housed in a building or set of buildings. Electronic technology has accelerated our pace away from that simple world to that of the twenty-first century. Here again we should resist the allure of exceptionalism. The printed catalogues of the nineteenth century and the card union catalogues of the first part of the twentieth century led to the rise of interlibrary lending (ILL) and borrowing and therefore extended the definition of "collection" to include material owned by other libraries and housed in distant places. These ILL arrangements grew in complexity and extent and really came into their own in the first phase of library automation that began in the late 1960s and flourished in the 1970s and 1980s. The ultimate expression of this was the gigantic union catalogue created by the OCLC (Online Computer Library Center). Area by area, state by state, and region by region, the complex net combining ILL agreements grew until it was quite reasonable to see the local collection as just a node (if the most important node to local users) of the national and international agglomeration of collections—a true library without walls before "virtual libraries" were dreamed of. Simultaneously, beginning in the late 1980s, libraries began to acquire and gain access to electronic documents of all sorts. They acquired or subscribed to documents on CD-ROMs and, with the growth of the Internet and the Web, gained access to huge numbers of electronic documents, websites, and resources—either free or by subscription.

The definition of a library collection has consequently expanded over the last 125 years to comprise at least four levels: locally owned physical documents; physical documents owned by other libraries but available through ILL; electronic documents that have been purchased or subscribed to; and "free" electronic documents.[6] It should be noted that each level is less organized and harder to gain systematic access to than its predecessor. Our collections have grown and evolved over a long period and it remains to be seen what the next evolutionary step will be. Not only should we understand the evolution of, not revolution in, library collections, but we should also eschew fashionable "end of history" notions about digital documents representing the ultimate in human communication. History and common sense tell us otherwise.

THE PEOPLE WHO WORK IN LIBRARIES

Our profession is changing in two important ways. We are older on average, and there is a knowledge gap between librarians educated in library schools 20 or more years ago and those of more recent vintage. In 1998, 57 percent of librarians in the United States were 45 years or older.[7] Using figures from the 1990 census, it is predicted that 58 percent of today's librarians will reach the age of 65 between 2005 and 2019.[8] These and other supporting data have so alarmed the federal government that it has proposed a $10 million initiative, administered by the Institute of Museum and Library Services, to recruit and educate a new generation of librarians. This laudable effort may well run up against societal forces flowing in the opposite direction (even if it survives recession-induced budget cuts). Librarians are growing older but so are the baby boomers (of which older librarians are only a tiny subset). The voting population is growing older, and so is the reading population (it is no coincidence that they are virtually coterminous). Similar data can be found on schoolteachers, university professors, and nurses.

The question that should haunt us is this: is librarianship just one example of the fact that today, older people tend to value education, learning, reading, the arts, and all the other traditional components of civilization more than young people? I ask this not as an old fogy lamenting the loss of imaginary golden ages (though that may be an accurate description), but as someone who has looked at all the statistics on the education, reading, voting, and other activities of cultivated and civic-minded people. The facts are there for anyone to read, and librarians alone cannot turn those tendencies around or change societal trends except as part of a broad cultural and educational coalition. Library and information science (LIS) schools are reporting that their students are very different demographically from the library school classes of twenty years ago. There are far fewer "traditional" students (holders of bachelor's degrees in their early to mid-twenties) and far more older people who are changing careers in midlife—spurred by the unavailability of jobs in academia, dislike of K–12 teaching, changes in their personal lives, and a myriad of other reasons. They are also attracted to library and information science (LIS) or information science (IS) schools by those schools' remarkably successful propaganda trumpeting the jobs that are supposedly available as an "information professional" in various nonlibrary settings. All this is a product of belief in the idea that we are in a unique and transformational time—an "information age" that calls for a complete revamping of library education or its abolition in favor of entirely new educational approaches.

The collapse of the dot.com companies and the puncturing of the information economy bubble have blunted the appeal of acquiring a master's degree in order to work as an "information professional," but unfortunately, it has not forced most LIS schools to rethink their curricula.

Let me state this as plainly and bluntly as I can: in the twenty-first century in America most LIS schools are not turning out graduates equipped with an education that will enable them to work in libraries successfully. I believe that, despite the propaganda, most LIS school students attend those schools with the intention of working in libraries of one kind or another. If they are to do that successfully, they need a thorough grounding in cataloguing, reference work, acquisitions and collection development, library instruction, specialized fields of librarianship (children's libraries, rare books, government documents, etc.), and other areas of practical work in libraries. Those LIS students who want to work outside libraries may need other areas of study (web page creation, communication theory, Java script, computer science, and whatnot), but why should the curriculum be skewed to that minority? The core library school curriculum varied little from the time Melvil Dewey established his library school until a mere twenty years ago. The courses surrounding that core changed over the years, as did the names of the core courses, but a discernible set of skills persisted over those 100 or more years. In the past quarter century, however, some of the successors to LIS schools have given up the idea of a core entirely (by not requiring their students to take library courses) and others have produced multiple-choice curricula that do not ensure a predictable product. The result is something that is an anomaly in a capitalist market-driven society. The consumers (library administrators) of the product (graduates) of LIS schools are asked to purchase (hire) that product without any attention being paid by the producers (LIS schools) to the needs and desires of the consumers. Any other marketer of products or supplier of services operating along those lines would have been out of business years ago.

The American Library Association's two conferences on professional education (in 1999 and 2000) created some initiatives—notably task forces on professional values and core competences—but have not come up with a plan to solve the many important issues that divide libraries and what passes for library education.[9] The fact that the two task forces had to struggle simply to reach a consensus on lists of our values and the skills and knowledge that define our profession speaks volumes about the pickle we are in. Would lawyers, doctors, clergy, or accountants have similar problems in defining their professions and the values that inspire them? Be that as it may, we need more than task forces and conferences to resolve this basic issue. We need a bold initiative to bring together library employers, librarians, library students, and those teachers in LIS schools who are interested in library education to reach agreement on the curricula that teachers want to teach, students want to study, and library employers agree will furnish the skills and knowledge that librarians need. If necessary, we need to create an association of library schools divorced from "information studies" and "information science." The latter disciplines may not believe their own propaganda enough to think they can survive the divorce—but that is scarcely our problem.

TECHNOLOGY IN LIBRARIES

Libraries have always been interested in and engaged with technology, both in terms of using modern technologies to support their programs and services and in engaging with new communications technologies. Libraries had compact shelving in the late nineteenth century, not to mention the latest typewriters, stereotyped catalogue cards, telephone reference service, and many other uses of the technologies of more than a century ago. In addition, each new form of communications technology, from microforms and phonograph records onward, has been adopted enthusiastically by libraries for the benefit of their users. Libraries' interest in technology accelerated in the years following the Second World War. Punched card systems and microcard systems were used for a variety of technical processing and retrieval purposes, particularly in the many special libraries that emerged during the 1940s and 1950s. That special library movement built, in turn, on the documentalist movement that began in the 1920s and 1930s. Each of these movements contributed a great deal to the scientific approach to library processes that changed librarianship in general.

Libraries were also early adopters of computers. Vannevar Bush was an influential figure for library school professors and students and library researchers in the postwar period.[10] His vision of "instruments" (computers) that would give "access to and command over the inherited knowledge of the ages" was compelling to all thinking librarians of the time. The profession was also greatly influenced (twenty years later) by a book written by the great computer scientist J. C. R. Licklider.[11] In his *Libraries of the Future*, Licklider foresaw networks, the idea of the interactive work space, and the ability of computers to allow users to connect to "everyday business, industrial, government, and professional information, and, perhaps, also to news, entertainment, and education." Licklider's ur-Web was a much more organized structure than the actual Web of forty years later, and a reading of his book demonstrates his grasp of the difference between knowledge and information—an understanding that is singularly lacking today. There are two striking things about his book. First, it was based on studies done and papers written in the early 1960s—long before serious computer applications in libraries. Second, the library profession enthusiastically embraced *Libraries of the Future* despite its having been written by an "outsider," a computer scientist at a time when hardly anyone had heard of such a specialty.

These early visions were followed in a few years by the creation of the MARC record, which had the paradoxical effects of, first, prolonging the life of the card catalogue by making card production more timely and efficient and, second, killing the card catalogue in the late 1970s and early 1980s. Computers became the basis of OCLC, of many homemade circulation systems, and of the earliest proprietary library systems.

There have been two periods in the Age of Computers in libraries. The first was that of library automation—the use of computers to make library processes such as circulation, cataloguing, serials control, and online searching more efficient. The second has been that of library digitization, in which some of the content accessed by means of libraries is found in digitized form and is stored and made accessible in computer systems. Library automation is so well established that the card catalogue and such artifacts as the Kardex seem as quaint as spinning jennies. Library digitization, by contrast, is in a muddled state and has an unpredictable future. It has built on the very considerable achievements of the library automation movement but has not carried on that movement's commitment to the computer as a tool. One notable example of this is the present generation of web-based catalogues, which are in many ways inferior not only to the first generation of OPACs but also to a well-maintained card catalogue. The central question that librarians must address (and which pervades the wider society as well as our own profession) is what happens when technology ceases to be a means to an end (library service) and becomes an end in itself? No serious person believes that, at a certain level of inquiry, resources available on the Web are superior to the contents of a well-run library, but many act as if it were so. By the phrase "a certain level of inquiry" I mean research that goes beyond the mere gathering of data and information. At that level, only a minute percentage of the world's recorded knowledge is available only on the Web, but college students don't believe this, and their consequent behavior is (at least tacitly) encouraged, when instead they should be taught the realities of the world of recorded knowledge, research, and serious inquiry.

PRESERVING THE HUMAN RECORD

Nicholson Baker has pursued his vendetta against librarians and library automation with such éclat that his minor celebrity status is assured.[12] The trouble is that there is some truth in his weird mishmash of nostalgia and generalizations from the particular. He did not like the online catalogue of a particular library;

therefore all online catalogues are bad. His lament for the penciled marginalia of the catalogue card was Baker at his most risible. He disputed (possibly correctly) the weeding policy of the San Francisco Public Library; ergo all librarians are vandals. Now he has discovered that some microfilming practices in newspaper libraries are less than adequate; therefore librarians hate paper. Alas, behind the polemics and accusations, there are some bleak truths. The human record *is* potentially endangered by digitization. The exceptionalism that has gripped some librarians *has* led them to discard material without thought for the needs of posterity. The existential panic made manifest in many conference papers and studies has created a climate in which Now (a present in which the speedy delivery of information is paramount) is catered to the exclusion of Then (the past in which the human record has been accumulating for centuries) and When (the future needs of our descendants for access to the human record as it is now). This is what lies at the heart of the appeal of Nicholson Baker and his ilk: a sense that librarians do not care anymore about their invaluable role as custodians, and a belief that the small-c conservatism that has characterized our profession is giving way to trendiness, electronic glitz, and instant gratification. I am convinced that most librarians are not in sympathy with such a betrayal of our historic role and achievements and will respond to any approach that integrates technology into our programs and services in an evolutionary manner.

NOTES

1. A. C. Grayling, *Meditations for the Humanist* (Oxford: Oxford University Press, 2002), 4.
2. Sacha Cohen, "At the Library, Finding Stacks of Pleasure," *Washington Post,* January 7, 2002, p. C9.
3. Alison Benjamin, "Read Alert," [London] *Guardian,* June 13, 2001.
4. Michael J. Crosbie and Damon D. Hickey, *When Change Is Set in Stone: An Analysis of Seven Academic Libraries Designed by Perry Dean Rogers, Architects* (Chicago: ACRL, 2001), 8–18.
5. Available at http://www.americaslibrary.gov.
6. For a discussion of what a "document" is, see chapter 8 of this book.
7. *Monthly Labor Review,* July 2000.
8. *American Libraries,* March 2002.
9. The first conference was held on April 30–May 1, 1999; see www.ala.org/congress/1st_congress.html. The second conference was held on November 17–19, 2000; see www.ala.org/congress2nd_congress.
10. Vannevar Bush, "As We May Think," *Atlantic Monthly* 176, no.1 (July 1945): 101–8.
11. J. C. R. Licklider, *Libraries of the Future* (Cambridge, Mass.: MIT Press, 1965).
12. Nicholson Baker, *Double Fold: Librarians and the Assault on Paper* (New York: Random House, 2001).

2 Communications Technology, 1875 to Now

*Moreover, this [the year 2000] will mark the end of a Platonic
Year consisting of twenty centuries—the Age of Pisces—and the
beginning of another, the Age of Aquarius. History and myth
converge at moments like this, and fears and expectations reach
a crescendo. As the rapidity of change accelerates, it becomes
evident that no one, not even the people best equipped with
the fastest computer networks, can register its myriad details,
let alone control them. The times rush ahead like a swollen
river, our destination directed by forces beyond our
understanding, never mind our control.
An end and a beginning are about to coincide.*[1]

MY READING OF HISTORY TELLS ME THAT, IN ALL AGES AND IN ALL PLACES, HUMAN BEINGS
labor under two delusions. They believe that they live in a time of unprecedented and transformational change and they believe in a lost, better, more
wholesome time that existed in happier days now gone forever. For every late
twentieth- or twenty-first-century prophet preaching the uniqueness of the "age
of information," there is a sixteenth, seventeenth, eighteenth, or nineteenth-
century equivalent extolling or bewailing the ways in which technological innovation was transforming his society. For every modern nostalgist who laments
the passing of the American society of the 1950s, there is a William Morris
mourning, in the last part of the nineteenth century, the passing of a lost age of

art and industry, and beauty without guilt.[2] It is odd that people, particularly Americans, can simultaneously hold an "onward and upward" belief in technology and a belief in a lost age of innocence. It is as though humanity is always being asked to balance material progress with moral regression and efficiency with a less satisfying way of life. There are shreds of truth in all this, but essentially both beliefs are delusions. The story of technology is not one of smooth, unalloyed progress, and not all innovations are beneficial. The contrary belief in the "good old days" is equally delusory. The acid test is to take a period being commended as belonging to that fabled time and read contemporary accounts of living then. The rose-tinted spectacles soon change to mundane clear glass. Carly Simon sang "These are the good old days," but does anyone really believe that to be more than a personal statement and the early 1970s to have been a glorious time?[3] Each of us lives in the single, shining moment of "now," but our lives are overwhelmingly made up of the past. We must understand that past and learn from it if we are to understand ourselves and our society, and in doing so, make progress.

One key to understanding the past is the knowledge that people then did not live in the past—they lived in the present, a present no less real and immediate to them than ours is to us. The present we are living in will be the past sooner than we might wish. What we perceive as its uniqueness will come to be seen as just a part of the past as viewed from the point of a future present that will in turn see itself as unique. People in history did not wear quaintly old-fashioned clothes—they wore modern clothes. They did not speak in archaic words and phrases—just as we do, they used or deprecated the most modern idioms. They did not see themselves as comparing unfavorably with the people of the future, they compared themselves and their lives favorably with the people of their past. In the context of our area of interest, it is particularly interesting to note that at no time in history have people seen themselves as technologically primitive. On the contrary, they always saw themselves as they were—at the leading edge of technology in what they thought of as a time of unprecedented change.

A LONG STORY

It has generally been accepted that human communications technology started with the "creative explosion" in what are now France and Spain about 40,000 years ago. Paintings and other markings found in celebrated caves indicate that the early humans of that period, having displaced the Neanderthals, had developed a capacity for abstract thought and, contemporaneously, the desire and ability to communicate it. It now appears that those capacities may have arisen considerably earlier in light of the discovery of intricate geometric carvings on seven pieces of ochre (a red stone) from a South African cave, those carvings being dated from 77,000 years ago.[4] Be that as it may, humankind has been communicating in language, images, and pictures for a very long time. It is salutary to note that, apart from a few carvings, cave paintings, and the like, we have no record of any of that communication before about 5,000 years ago. This means that depending on the time at which the "creative explosion" took place, we have an (often fragmentary) knowledge of only one-tenth to one-fifteenth of the total time span of human communication. (See figure 2.1.) Looked at in this

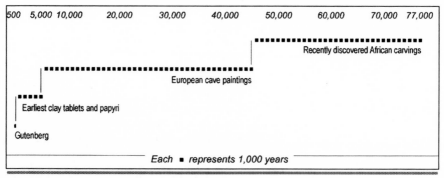

FIGURE 2.1   Time Line of Early Communications Technology

light, we *are* in an exceptional time, one characterized by an explosion of communication and creativity, profound changes in society, and a transformation of civilization and culture. This exceptional time began in the mid-fifteenth century and shows no sign of relapsing or abating. However, we should try to avoid confusion between advances in the technology by which messages are conveyed and advances in the content carried by that technology. E-mail is technologically superior to the use of pen and ink and writing paper for personal communication. Does anyone believe that the content of e-mail messages is superior to the content of the pen-and-ink letters of yesteryear? Television is vastly more technologically advanced than the live theater. With a very few shining exceptions, there is no excellent television drama, whereas the live theater continues to flourish as it has for centuries.

THE "INFORMATION REVOLUTION"

Taking a shorter view of communications technology, the Copernican theory tells us it is extremely unlikely that this is a time of an unprecedented "information revolution" or similarly transformational event.[5] This has not prevented masses of overheated rhetoric, of which the following is a sample (from among thousands of such pronouncements):

> The truly revolutionary impact of the Information Revolution is just beginning to be felt. But it is not "information" that fuels this impact. It is not "artificial intelligence." It is not the effect of computers and data processing on decision-making, policymaking, or strategy. It is something that practically no one foresaw or, indeed, even talked about ten or fifteen years ago: e-commerce— that is, the explosive emergence of the Internet as a major, perhaps eventually the major, worldwide distribution channel for goods, for services, and, surprisingly, for managerial and professional jobs. This is profoundly changing economies, markets, and industry structures; products and services and their flow; consumer segmentation, consumer values, and consumer behavior; jobs and labor markets. But the impact may be even greater on societies and politics and, above all, on the way we see the world and ourselves in it.[6]

The author, Peter Drucker, was of course, writing in the dim distant days of the penultimate year of the last century, but note the casual assumption that there is something called an "Information Revolution" whose impact, true to form for such writings, has yet to be felt fully. Transformational change is always just around the corner for the likes of Drucker, and they are strangers to the injunction that "tomorrow never comes." We will pass over the idea that e-commerce would be the engine of the coming transformation, since even a futurist of Drucker's eminence could not foresee the three cruel years that technology-based companies would endure shortly after his article was published in 1999. If you are in the futurism business, though, you should understand that it is natural for us lesser mortals to expect some prescience—it is, after all, your stock in trade. Still less should we dwell on the apparently fatuous idea that the Internet would be the "major distribution channel" for managerial and professional jobs. I say "apparently fatuous" because it is not at all clear exactly what the author means, but his belief that something terrific and unprecedented is happening is patent.

Even the estimable Carnegie Endowment for International Peace is engaged on a major "Information Revolution and World Politics" project.[7] It seeks to analyze "the political, economic, and social dimensions of the worldwide Information Revolution and their implications for U.S. policy and global governance." All the constituents of the project are worthy and informative, but one doubts if any of them would be funded if they were not wrapped in the exceptionalism of an "Information Revolution." I could cite many more such writings and projects in support of the received wisdom that this is a unique time with unique challenges, but wish only to state that there is no reading of history that supports this lurid view. In the words of Brian Winston, "What is hyperbolised as a revolutionary train of events can be seen as a far more evolutionary and less transforming process."[8] Furthermore, it is my belief that the exceptionalist view itself is inimical to considered thought and action on the real problems we do face. Those seized with the idea of exceptionalism tend to abandon rational analysis, tend to have misplaced priorities when allocating resources, and tend to have a naive belief that the latest thing is always to be preferred to established policies and procedures. The disappointments experienced by those who hold the latter view arise from the fact that there is always a new latest thing and last month's latest thing has to yield to it.

A HUNDRED YEARS

There are peaks and valleys in the ever-evolving history of technology and society, and our present situation is foreshadowed by technological innovations over centuries. Much of our cutting-edge technology is the logical and natural outcome of ideas that are decades, even centuries, old. Here we are in the earliest years of the twenty-first century. I want to begin my analysis of our present and future by speaking of the people of the earliest years of the twentieth century, and the difference between their lives and ours. When a person of the year 2103 looks back at the quaint old world of 2003, she will probably see a gigantic gulf between then and now, one that will seem much greater than the differences between now and 1903. However that may be, here we are, trapped in our present, peering at the future as in a glass darkly, but able to look back with clarity because libraries have preserved the records of humankind. This last is no light statement; in fact, it has enormous weight behind it. It cannot be overstressed that libraries and librarians are the sole reason why we have that clarity of backward vision. We know almost all there is to know about a century ago (and far earlier) largely because the thoughts, actions, and creativity of our ancestors were recorded in print on paper, and the resulting books and journals were acquired, stored, and preserved by libraries. If a significant part of the thoughts, actions, and creativity of people today and in the immediate future is available only in digital form, that comprehensive knowledge of the past is in jeopardy. Unless major and innovative steps are taken, it is highly unlikely that a person living a century from now will have the ability to read, view, and hear the records of today and tomorrow. This potential cultural catastrophe cannot be underplayed. Great writers and thinkers will find a way to reach a global audience whatever happens to print on paper and digitized documents. However, for every such person, there are tens of thousands of others who also contribute to our culture and the human record. Their work and ideas will survive only if they are recorded in a robust format with great longevity. No amount of cyber blue smoke and mirrors can obscure the fact that the *only* such technology we know is print on paper, especially the printed book. Other formats are either manifestly fallible (film, microforms, etc.) or untested by time (electronic documents). The latter may prove durable over the centuries, but that is a highly optimistic basis for a cultural gamble with grave consequences. (See chapters 8 and 9 for further examination of these points.)

TECHNOLOGY OVER THE LAST 150 YEARS

Technology had been producing marvels in the twenty-five years before the start of the twentieth century. It is notable that a comprehensive list of innovations and inventions shows that almost all of them came from one of four countries— the United States, the United Kingdom, France, and Germany—divided almost equally.[9] In preparation for a century of movement, the 1890s saw the introduction of the electric bicycle, underground electric railway, diesel engine, motorcycle, outboard engine, gasoline-powered truck, gearbox, motor barge, motor bus, electric bus, speedometer, taxi, and rigid airship, as well as many of the inventions that made possible airplanes and the mass production of automobiles. In a scant few decades, these transportation inventions alone would change the world, for good and ill, to an extent that appeared to those living at the time to be unprecedented and transformational. This revolution in locomotion was arguably at least as far-reaching in its global effect as the computer revolution is today.

The 1890s also produced the aluminum saucepan, machine gun, premature baby incubator, vacuum flask, domestic electric fire, milking machine, X-rays, dial telephone, ice cream cone, aspirin, high-speed steel production, paper clip, hearing aid, and safety razor. These and countless other innovations transformed the domestic and working lives of almost everyone in the world. The transformation was faster and mainly benign in western European countries and North America, and was slower and often malign in the colonies and less economically advanced countries of Africa, Asia, and Latin America. In these regions, it was the Western technological advantage (principally in locomotion, communications, and military technology) that made possible the subjugation and exploitation of what we now call the Third World. We are still living with the fallout of that technological dominance used for amoral and racist ends.

Technology was beginning to exert a great influence on the material lives of Americans in 1901, but it was also preparing to exert a great influence over their interior lives.

Letter writing was very common at the turn of the century (and was just one indication of a higher level of applied literacy then than now). This high level of communication was made possible by three technological innovations—the mass-produced lead pencil (1890s), the fountain pen (first manufactured in 1884), and the mass production and wide availability of inexpensive writing paper.[10]

An astonishing variety of printed serial publications was available to the reader of 1901. It is well known that large American cities had numerous morning and afternoon newspapers (many in languages other than English) and that there were also many weekly and monthly magazines. It is less well known that equally large numbers of magazines and newspapers with a broad readership were published in small towns and rural areas. Though there were then as now, *mutatis mutandis,* scandal sheets and popular tabloids, the level of literacy needed to ingest the texts of most serial publications then was far higher than is required by their modern counterparts.

The age of mass photography was in full swing. Modern photography began in 1887, when George Eastman replaced glass photographic plates with celluloid—also a necessary precondition of moving pictures. He introduced the Brownie camera ("Pull the string, turn the key, press the button") in 1888 and everyone could take pictures of his or her family, friends, surroundings, and vacations with no training or skill required. In the course of time, the family photograph album replaced the family Bible and the packet of scented letters tied in purple ribbon as the fundamental chronicle of individuals and their relatives.

America in 1901 was full of visual stimulation. Magazines were heavily illustrated and contained graphic advertisements. Cheap reproductions of artworks, battle scenes, portraits, and religious scenes hung in every parlor. Posters and placards decorated almost every public place. Postcards, photographs, calendars, greeting cards, and many other graphic media were everywhere to be found. Stereoscopes and 3-D stereo cards were as common in living rooms as televisions are today. This abundance of visuality was made possible by the mass-production application of new technologies. This abundance of visuality still exists and has been enhanced by the ubiquity of electronic images on television, in films, and on the Internet. In addition, the presence of sound in almost every public and private place adds another dimension of stimulation.

The first central telephone exchange was established in 1878 in New Haven, Connecticut (in an office that also issued the first telephone directory). By 1901, long distance telephony was a well-established technology. In 1893, the Bell Company leased telephones to 260,000 customers (one for every 250 people in the United States).[11] Here we have the beginnings of a telephone network that is today the greatest communications network the world has ever seen, far surpassing the Internet in its ubiquity and in its effect on human lives.[12] Nowadays, when calling someone in Australia or India is a commonplace act, it is hard to imagine the change that telephony wrought in the lives of people and in the doings of society.

In 1877 Thomas Edison demonstrated the first version of the phonograph. Within a very few years, a subsidiary of the Edison Company installed "nickel in the slot" phonographs in soda fountains and saloons, ending the careers of many saloon piano players. Emile Berliner developed the flat-disc phonograph "record" in 1896. These developments meant that for the first time in history, a permanent record of musical performances and human speech was possible, something that, when realized, revolutionized both historical studies and musicology as well as popular entertainment.

By the 1890s, three main kinds of high-quality printing—rotary letterpress, rotogravure, and metal plate lithography—were in common use.[13] Their effects on the mass production of printed texts and images were profound and far-reaching.

Microfilms were used in the Franco-Prussian War of 1870. They became a standard part of library economy without ever pleasing the great majority of library users or providing (as the more hyperactive modernizers of the 1950s thought) the ultimate answer to library space problems.

The 1890s also saw the appearance of the kinematograph camera and projector and photographic typesetting (all the invention of the remarkable Englishman William Friese-Greene), the cylindrical cipher machine, telephoto lens, portable typewriter, film studio, language-teaching courses on wax cylinders, wireless telegraphy, ciné film show (the first movies), photogravure, "visible typewriter" (one on which the typist could see what she was typing), cathode ray tube, pianola, loudspeaker, tape recorder, "cineorama" (which used ten projectors), and electric typewriter.[14]

In 1901 Reginald Fessenden designed the heterodyne receiver, a device that made radio possible.[15] In June 1908, the British electrical pioneer Campbell Swinton published a letter in *Nature* that laid down "the basic principle of modern television."[16]

These innovations, in Thomas Schlereth's words, "stimulated what many historians regard as a 'communications revolution.'"[17] He quotes Warren Sussman: "Consciousness itself was altered. The very perception of time and space was radically changed."[18] These words could be and are used by pundits and sages today concerning the cyberfuture. There are many such apocalyptic visions among the writings and speeches of our time, such as this proclamation of a new Renaissance:

> [T]he theme really is Renaissance 2.0, as I call it. It has the concept that we are about to approach a new age of enlightenment or a new age of learning and knowledge. Because of the telecommunications developments that have occurred recently, and this will, though it may sound presumptuous and a lot of hype, lead to a new age of civilization perhaps.[19]

This really is a bit over the top. When you think of the efflorescence of learning, creativity, and civilization that occurred in the real Renaissance, such a statement verges on the simple-minded. Epochal comments of this type did not begin just 100 years ago—a Philadelphia newspaper proclaimed in 1844 that its "Telegraphic News" section was "the annihilation of space."[20] Despite these dreams and fantasies, the fact is that almost every technology used in human communication today was present in at least embryonic form in the first year of the twentieth century. The computer is a possible, but not complete exception—since the concept of the computer can clearly be seen in the writings and work of Charles Babbage (1791–1871) in the first half of the nineteenth century.[21] The tremendous impact of the innovations of the late nineteenth century was at least comparable to what the radio, television, computer, and other recent innovations have done to communications and human life in the last twenty years. The point here is not to make cheap and easy points about the overblown nature of today's forecasts, but to show that we belong to a continuum of achievement, that we must understand that continuum and our place in it, and that rational appraisal will serve us better than overheated rhetoric that lacks a factual or even plausible foundation.

The Americans of 1901 had a relatively low level of exposure to the diversions and distractions that absorb so much of our time today. This was partly due to fact that much infotainment technology had yet to be invented, but it was due far more to socioeconomic realities. The United States had made significant breaks with the traditional structures of European society but was far from a classless society. There was a relatively small minority of people with the time and money to pursue culture and frivolous distractions and entertainment. The vast mass of people had neither the money nor the time for such diversions, high or low. For them life was hard, whether in a big city, in mill towns, or in the country. Workdays began early and ended late, hence the time for both study and entertainment was limited. Technologically speaking, there was no close analogue to watching sports on fifty-inch television screens, surfing the Web, listening to Walkmen, using mobile phones and computer devices, playing video games, or many other technologically advanced recreations. Other diversions of the late nineteenth and early twentieth centuries have close analogues today—for example, the life of the modern shopping mall is not markedly different from the life of the town or village square a century ago. The consumerism and materialism that pervade life today were only in a fledgling state. The population was still mostly rural—though the great cities of America teemed with poor and huddled masses of immigrants—and life centered on small communities and neighborhoods, with three generations of the same family living in proximity or in the same dwelling. Far fewer people than now had access to education beyond the elementary level, and the proportion of people who were literate in the narrow sense of being able to read was far lower than it is today. However, if by "literacy" one means the ability to engage in, and the practice of, sustained reading of complex texts, it is very doubtful that we live in a more literate society today. On the other hand, standards of health and nutrition were at a far lower level than they are now, and life expectancy since then has increased greatly, due in large part to science and technology.

Our lives today are suffused with creature comforts beyond the dreams of even the wealthiest people of a century ago, and the amount of information potentially available to almost everyone today is also far greater now. It is even arguable that we possess more knowledge today than our ancestors of the late nineteenth century did, though we have to acknowledge that most of that new knowledge is scientific, technical, and medical—practical in intent and in its products. Do we really *know* more now about the meaning of life, the nature of humankind, and the mysteries of the human heart and soul? Are the literature and art of today superior to that of the beginning of the last century? In a world saturated with information and data, are we more knowledgeable or merely more informed? What is the nature of human life today if, crammed with statistics and factoids, we know thousands of trees but have no knowledge of the infinite forest in which we, our ancestors, and our descendants live, whether we and they like it or not?

TECHNOLOGY IN LIBRARIES 100 YEARS AGO

Today many equate technology with computer technology, and all the preceding ways in which men and women used machines to ease labor and be more productive seem unimportant. The fact is that library life a century ago was by no means unaffected by technology. The following are a set of examples drawn from the text of advertisements in the *Library Journal* issues of the day.

> In April 1900, F. M. Crunden of the St. Louis Public Library reported with some satisfaction on his comparison of the Remington, Hammond, and Smith-Premier typewriters, with preference for the Remington, not least because it furnished "a complete card attachment, which works easily and satisfactorily." In contradiction of Mr. Crunden, an advertisement for the Hammond typewriter in September 1900 stressed that it has "a special library type, and furthermore prints in any language, style of type or color of ink . . ." No one stepped forward as an advocate for the Smith-Premier.

> J. Rufus Wales of Marlboro, Massachusetts, advertised his patented improved spring back bookbinding system in January 1901. Library users of the time had fewer books from which to choose and the small collections of many libraries had very high volume/usage ratios—hence the need for inexpensive and efficient binding systems

> The American Library Association exhibit at the Paris Exposition of 1900 contained examples of eleven different circulation systems; many styles of printed catalogue card; twenty styles of temporary binders; specimen volumes for the blind printed in New York point, American Braille, Boston line letter, and Moon; and "the travel stained case and well worn books of the Stout travelling library, no. 26, both making clearer than many words the full meaning of the new spirit of American librarianship."[22] The traveling library was an attempt to bring books to people no matter where they lived. The fact that the volumes were "well worn" is a testament to the thirst for reading and the success of the traveling concept.

> No less a light than Charles Ammi Cutter gave advice on the acquisition, cataloguing, display, and preservation of photographs and photoprints in October 1900 at the Montreal Annual Conference of the ALA. He

noted the way in which the "most advanced libraries" had been laying in large collections of photographs and gave his opinion that photographs are to art what concerts are to music. Three-quarters of a century before the idea of the "media center" took hold, one of the great minds of American librarianship was not only aware of the value of image collections but also had formulated practices for making them available and useful.

Shelving systems (including moveable systems) abounded, and the Art Metal Construction Company, maker of the reliable Fenton Steel Stacks, was a frequent *Library Journal* advertiser.

The Library of Congress's Bernard Green presented a paper on the planning and construction of library buildings (March 1900) that gives a fine illustration of the dizzying pace of change at the time. He described the small, dreary libraries of a few decades before and went on:

> Books have increased and multiplied almost beyond comprehension both in number and diversity . . . . Periodical and newspaper literature may yet swamp the world in print. The earth and the heavens are being traversed and surveyed extensively and the growth and value of maps and charts has already become voluminous . . . . Manuscripts are being collected and extensively studied and collated, requiring accommodations in safe, specially constructed cases, while prints and the graphic art of illustration . . . have kept pace with and become an invaluable adjunct of the printed book.

Green went on to discuss the "special mechanical devices" such as automatic book carriers, pneumatic tubes for delivering messages, and electric signals that enabled the Library of Congress to deliver a book from its shelves to a reader within four minutes of receiving a request.

In June 1908, John Fretwell reported on "photographic copying in libraries" based on work done in Germany by a Professor Krumbacher. He concentrated on the production of facsimiles of the book and manuscript holdings of great libraries and the copying of illustrations. There were many different methods available at the time, variously involving the use of a stereopticon, glass plates, bromide paper, orthochromatic emulsions, and reversing prisms. The impression one gains of Herr Doktor Krumbacher is one of a teeming, technologically oriented mind and a relentless bent for innovation.

Many letters, communications, and editorials in the *Library Journal* in the earliest years of the twentieth century were concerned with new techniques, methods, and applications of machinery. The same articles and pages also carry much rumination on the implications of what the authors saw as a great rate of change in the profession and in library service to a growing and changing population. The tone of these articles is very similar to the tone of articles today. Will libraries and librarianship survive? Will growth in the diversity and number of means of communication change libraries for the better or for the worse? Will a changing society value libraries in the future? All these questions we ask today were being asked 100 years ago. I will look at the present state of libraries in the next chapter, mindful of the fact that we have traveled a long road, but it is still the same road and we owe much to those who traveled it before us.

NOTES

1. Murray Stein, *Transformation* (College Station: Texas A&M University Press, 1998).
2. The 1950s in America were a period conspicuous for the oppression of minorities and women and the suppression of intellectual freedom, savagely criticized by many thinkers of the time.
3. Carly Simon, "Anticipation," 1971.
4. *Los Angeles Times,* January 11, 2002.
5. J. Richard Gott, quoted by Timothy Ferris in "How to Predict Everything," *New Yorker,* July 12, 1999, 35–39.
6. Peter F. Drucker, "Beyond the Information Revolution," *Atlantic Monthly* (digital edition), October 1999.
7. See www.ceip.org/files/projectsirwp/irwp_home..ASP.
8. Brian Winston, *Media Technology and Society* (London, New York: Routledge, 1998), 1.
9. Kevin Desmond, *Timetable of Inventions and Discoveries* (New York: M. Evans, 1986).
10. Many of the facts in this section are taken from chapter 5 of Thomas J. Schlereth, *Victorian America* (New York: HarperCollins, 1991).
11. Ruth Schwartz Cowan, *A Social History of American Technology* (Oxford: Oxford University Press, 1997), 160.
12. Winston, *Media Technology,* 336.
13. James Moran, "Printing," in *A History of Technology,* ed. Trevor I. Williams (Oxford: Clarendon, 1978), 7:1268.
14. Ray Allister, *Friese-Greene: Close-up of an Inventor* (New York: Arno, 1972).
15. Cowan, *American Technology,* 275–76.
16. Winston, *Media Technology,* 91.
17. Schlereth, *Victorian America,* 171.
18. Warren Sussman, *Culture as History* (New York: Pantheon, 1984).
19. Dennis Fazio, verbatim transcript of a presentation at "The Great Internet Transformation: The Telecommunications and Information Society Forum" (April 26, 2000), available at www.hhh.umn.edu/projects/tisp/042600.pdf.
20. Schlereth, *Victorian America,* 187.
21. Doron Swade, *The Difference Engine: Charles Babbage and the Quest to Build the First Computer* (New York: Viking, 2001).
22. Florence Woodworth, "ALA Exhibit at Paris Exposition of 1900," *Library Journal* 25, no. 3 (March 1900).

3   Communications Technology and Libraries Today

Britain's libraries have been locked in a downward spiral so long that it's hard to remember that they were once regarded as a vital national institution, just as much part of an ambitious city's civic arsenal as a successful art gallery is today . . . . [Libraries have] . . . become the preserve of the old and the disturbed . . . . A generation of book hating, self-loathing librarians, nervous of literature and hypnotised by technology, combined with uninspired local authorities who do not value their services, has only made things worse.[1]

THIS HARSH INDICTMENT OF BRITISH LIBRARIANS BY A RESPECTED ARCHITECTURAL CRITIC (in an essay celebrating a new public library) could also be applied, with some truth, to many American librarians. It does sometimes seem as if a one-time bookish profession has embraced technology to the point that Internet resources are viewed as actually being preferable to books, which are becoming increasingly irrelevant. The sad decline of the British public library from a national ornament to "the preserve of the old and disturbed" has many causes, but the alienation of the library profession from the values of learning, culture, and civilization is one of them. If we are to come to terms with modern communications technology without losing our souls, we must see the role and nature of that technology clearly. Perhaps you might see these words as apocalyptic and overheated. If so, consider this pronouncement on academic libraries by an eminent figure in the field of "library and information management":

I have been amazed at how infrequently I need to use my university's library . . . That is not to say that I don't use library services. I do, and frequently, but almost always from my desktop—or rather from my laptop. I work from home, from the train, from hotels, from partner institutions, and even occasionally from my office . . .[2]

Now, if an eminent "information manager" has fallen for the idea that all useful documents ("information resources" in his jargon) are available electronically, what chance does the average person have in dealing with this preposterous idea? If what seems to be high-level research (the author is director of something called the Centre for Research in Library and Information Management) can be confined to digital documents, surely lower-level needs can be met from computer resources alone? I suppose one could trust in common sense and experience to demonstrate that such opinions are not only fallacious but dangerous. Opinions such as these are a threat to the funding of libraries and the livelihoods of librarians. Lest the latter be misinterpreted as merely part of a job-protection program, I hasten to add that the employment of librarians is vital to society and culture because the skills they have and the service ethic they embody are invaluable and irreplaceable. I have been accused in the past of tilting at windmills and straw men (I'm not sure that straw men are what one tilts at, but there we are) but never, to my knowledge, by anyone who works in a library and who knows about the real pressures exerted by misinformed purse-holders.[3] The nightmare of most working librarians is a university administrator, a chair of a public library board, or a school trustee who sincerely believes that "everything is available on the Internet" and the digital library is just around the corner. Ignorance and lazy thinking fuel such beliefs, but they are also reinforced by writings, usually emanating from people qualified in fields other than librarianship.

THE STRANGE CASE OF DR. ARMS

Take the case of William Y. Arms, professor of computing at Cornell University and a self-appointed expert on digital libraries. In a remarkable paper, ostensibly on libraries, published in 2000, Arms displays the combination of arrogance and ignorance that is characteristic of his type.[4] According to him,

Progress is being made in reducing material[s] costs. Open access materials on the Internet are making many primary materials available at no cost. (p. 1)

Oh, really? What is the percentage of scholarly materials that are available on the Internet at no cost? How many of them are derived from the print industry?

All we get are hand-waving and vagueness from Professor Arms, because his real target—having disposed, to his satisfaction, of the inconvenient facts of the cost of scholarly books and journals—is the role of the librarian and how to get rid of the latter:

> If professional and research information is to be available more widely, either users will have to bypass libraries, or libraries will have to employ fewer people. (p. 2)

Having delivered himself of this magisterial non sequitur, Arms goes on to talk about the tasks of librarians (always to him "professional librarians," presumably to distinguish them from amateur librarians) and how computers could perform them. He starts with cataloguing and an attempt at equivalence between library cataloguing and search engines. He admits that "almost everything that is best about a library catalog service is done badly by a web search service," but hastens to add that web indexing services are cheap and cover more documents than library catalogues. This argument beggars belief. It would be far cheaper to have surgery performed by your brother-in-law Fred armed with a saw and instructions from the Internet than it would be to go to the Mayo Clinic (another institution with high labor costs). Also, once he got into the swing of it, Fred could probably perform many more operations than a team of surgeons at the Mayo Clinic.

Arms then compares Google to Inspec (the indexing/abstracting service for computer science), with a tip of his hat to the former. The history of indexing is littered with scientists and technologists making generalizations based on their own disciplines, while conveniently ignoring the problems of vocabulary in the social sciences and humanities. He compounds this elementary error:

> But its [Google's] greatest strength is that everything in its indexes is available online with open access . . . . Inspec references [sic] a formally published version, which is usually printed or online with restricted access. (p. 3)

So there we are. Google is "better" than Inspec because everything to which it gives access is online and costs nothing. Perhaps you can find everything that you need in computer science online and free. However, in the vast majority of disciplines, serious research and scholarship are not possible without access to "formally published versions" in print or online by subscription.

Arms goes on to question the future of reference librarians and grudgingly comes to the conclusion that "nothing on the horizon approaches human judgement in understanding such subtleties" (p. 8). He remains confident that this is a transient phase, and that although there are "tough technical and organizational problems" ahead, there is "nothing that cannot be solved in twenty years of natural evolution" (p. 8). He concludes that not only will automated digital libraries replace real libraries, but also that librarians have no skills that can be used to help in achieving this happy state of affairs.

Arms's paper is dotted with laudatory references to Google and the power and authority of its search algorithms. It is therefore pertinent to note that a Google search using "William Arms" yields "about 1,350" results in no useful order, and though the good professor's home page is the first thing retrieved, the first ten results (deemed by Google's powerful algorithms to be the most relevant) include the coat of arms of a prince of the British royal family; symbols of the city of Thunder Bay, Canada; and miscellaneous songs by one William Arms Fisher. Bizarrely, refining the search to "William Y. Arms" yields 1,460 results (110 more than the coarser search). Since they too are in no useful order, I could not check them all and can only assume they all relate to our Professor Arms and, therefore, must include relevant items not retrieved by Google's algorithms on the first search. "William Yeo Arms" yields "about 34" results. Librarians may be about to pass from the stage of history, but we do know a little bit about vocabulary control, relevance, and recall in indexing, and arranging search results in a useful order. Please note that these searches are in the relatively orderly world of personal names and do not involve the complexities of free-text searching versus controlled subject searching or the even more freakish results of the former.

The reader may be asking why I have devoted a number of paragraphs to one article by one person. The answer is that he is one of many, unfortunately influential, people who speak and write against the interests of real libraries. No straw man he—this consultant to the Library of Congress, influential member of the National Research Council and other gatherings of the great, and author of *Digital Libraries*.[5] No doubt it is only a matter of time before he is invited to an ALA conference to tell us how outmoded we are. Certainly, it will be far longer before a "professional librarian" is invited to a computer science conference to tell them how passé they are and how misguided their endeavors.

COMMUNICATIONS TECHNOLOGY

The history of communications technology shows us that though types of communication *within* media may rise and fall, broad categories of communications media do not go out of existence. This is at the heart of the discussion about the future of libraries. There are, broadly speaking, three schools of thought. There are those who think that digital media, in defiance of history or the needs of consumers, will overwhelm all other media, and hence libraries as we know them have no future. There are those who believe that digital media will come to dominate, but not obliterate, all other communications media, and therefore libraries will undergo a sea change—persisting but in an increasingly unrecognizable form. Finally, there are those who believe that we are at an interesting point in the evolution of communications media—a point at which digital media will find their place and level in society and will be incorporated into the ever-evolving library. The fundamental theory behind this book—that we do not live in a transformational time—leads me to the third opinion. Our friend Dr. Arms is evidently of the first persuasion. Using the time-hallowed trick of presenting opinions as questions that necessitate no supporting facts or even logic, he presents us with the following remarkable passage:

> Conventional wisdom states that new technology supplements the old but does not replace it. This view implies that digital libraries will coexist with traditional materials forever. But is this assumption justified? Does it obstruct our willingness to be really creative in our research? In fact history shows that new technology can drive out the old. Consider, for example, typewriters and gramophone records. Ten years after the introduction of superior technology, both were essentially dead. Where I work, the U.S. mail is following the same track to oblivion. If the mail service suddenly ceased, we would hardly notice; it has been replaced by e-mail.[6]

It is a fact not always universally acknowledged that much conventional wisdom is correct. History tells us that new communications technology does, in truth, supplement and enhance the old and no amount of "creative research" can obscure that fact. The idea that the replacement of typewriters by word processors and LPs by CDs are examples of old technologies being killed by new technologies verges on the inane. Word processors are essentially electronic typewriters with capabilities that exceed the Selectric by about the same degree as the Selectric's exceeded a Remington of the 1920s. The CD displacing the LP is less significant than the flat-disc sound recording displacing the wax cylinder and the wire. Modern automobiles are equipped with a multiplicity of electronics and computer capabilities. That does not make my 2001 Chevy Malibu a new technology displacing the Chevy Bel Air of the 1950s. Each of these examples is a refinement within a particular technology, employing electronics and computers. That Arms's argument is bolstered with such weak examples is an indicator of the strength of the conventional wisdom. I am not greatly familiar with Ithaca, New York, but what an odd place it must be if its inhabitants would not notice the disappearance of the U.S. postal service. Had radio been abolished, and not transformed, by television, or if the Vietnam memorial in Washington, D.C., were a laser installation instead of carvings on stone, Dr. Arms would have a strong case for his argument by questions. Since nothing like that can be adduced, he has no case at all.

Now for a last quotation from Dr. Arms. Here his pseudo-questions betray his true objectives:

> Can we envisage a . . . transmogrification of libraries, in which the old structures disappear, but some of the essence remains? If so, what might disappear? Library buildings are expensive; they could disappear from university campuses. Scientific journals are in a period of rapid change. What evidence do we have that journals are a cost-effective way to serve the research community in an electronic world? Over time, scientific journals could cease to be physical artifacts on paper, published by traditional organizations. With cuts in government expenditures and government web sites, do we need the Government Printing Office? Should the Library of Congress celebrate the new millennium with an announcement that it will become purely digital?[7]

Perhaps Dr. Arms is trying to shock, or perhaps the last sentence is an example of the dry wit for which computer scientists are famous. The alert reader will note the clever mixing of the feasible with the incredible, a trope that seeks to equate the latter with the former. Vandals and Goths seek the removal of useful buildings that are symbols of learning and civilization, but one need be neither to question the present framework of scholarly communication, particularly in the sciences. Similarly, only an ignoramus or joker could call for the digitization of the Library of Congress, but the fact that the Government Printing Office is in jeopardy is well known.[8] The vast majority of the LC's collections are not digitized and never will be digitized (for practical and economic reasons), whereas almost all U.S. government publications are already in digital form. The debate over the role of the Government Printing Office has nothing to do with the established facts of technology, but rather with the dispute over the distribution of the government information for which we have all paid.

BUDGETS AND PRIORITIES

Libraries use a variety of technologies to acquire, give access to, disseminate, and preserve recorded knowledge and information. The diversity of libraries (even those in the same system) ensures that the percentages of holdings in various media and the expenditures on those media will vary greatly from one library to another. This is most evident in the case of the balance between print and digital collections, but it also applies to other media. A public library will spend far more proportionally on videotapes and DVDs than almost any academic library. School and curriculum libraries will purchase a large number of kits. Even within one technology, there are different priorities; for example, a specialized scientific, technical, or medical library will spend far more on serial literature than on books. The one unifying principle is found in the library's budget—the expression of the perceived or actual desires and needs of its users. It is possible to argue that those needs and desires should not be the sole drivers of the agenda. Again it depends on the kind of library. A major research library has an eye on posterity and builds collections for the ages—something that may be in conflict with some of today's needs. A middle-sized public library takes, quite correctly, a far more short-term view and is more concerned with meeting today's needs and the demands of today's users.

THE LANDSCAPE TODAY

Most libraries deal with a mix of communication technologies. There are instances in which this is not true—rare book collections, sound recording libraries, digital services in specialized scientific, technical, or medical areas, etc.—but for the great majority of libraries the question is not whether to deal with such a mix but in which proportion and at which price. While there is much talk of digital libraries and the paramount significance and importance of the Web, the figures for other media are seldom mentioned.

Books

Take the case of books.

In 1999 (the last year for which firm figures are available):
- there were 53,109 hardback titles published in the United States
- there were 66,248 paperback titles published in the U.S.
- there were 9,438 children's books published in the U.S.

In 2000 (the last year for which firm figures are available):
- the U.S. imported 851,850,000 volumes from other countries
- the U.S. imported 6,239,699 scientific, technical, and professional volumes from the United Kingdom alone[9]

There are many more statistics that illustrate the health and extent of the book trade, but these few show that even if libraries confined themselves to current U.S. publications, books are destined to remain a significant element of their collections.

The OCLC WorldCat contained 38,445,556 records for books in October 2001.[10] These records constitute 83.87 percent of the database, but significant numbers of other materials can also be found. (It should be noted that, at least in theory, OCLC contains only one record for each title or document.) The database also contains records for:

- 2,283,000 serials
- 1,400,000 "visual materials"
- More than 630,000 maps
- 310,000 "mixed materials"
- 1,546,000 sound recordings
- More than 1,000,000 scores[11]

A look at publishing in other "non-book" areas yields similarly impressive figures. (Please note that it is not possible to come up with exactly, or even roughly, comparable statistics across the media.)

Serials

Definitive statistics on periodicals and other types of serial literature are notoriously difficult to compile and analyze because of the problems in defining such terms as "journal," "magazine," "serial," and "periodical," and because of the overlap between these and other designations. One authoritative source yields the following (note that these figures do not include annuals, almanacs, etc.):

There are more than 75,000 periodical titles currently published in the United States and Canada. The numbers in some selected areas are:

- agriculture: 920 titles
- education: 2,332 titles
- library and information science: 718 titles
- newspapers: 6,155 titles
- religion and theology: 2,042 titles.[12]

The *National Directory of Magazines* tells us that there were 17,694 magazine titles published in the United States in 2001.[13]

Ulrich's says that in 2001 there were 20,430 active online journals, but of those, only 2,040 were available solely in electronic form (almost 10 percent)—the others being analogues of print journals.[14]

Sound Recordings

In 1999, 38,900 new sound recordings were issued in the United States (up from 18,400 in 1992).[15] These represent only titles (for example, a release on tape cassette and CD is counted as one release). A *Billboard* correspondent laments the glut of content, stating that the 35,516 new albums, including a preponderance of independent labels, had saturated the market.[16]

Video Recordings

According to the *International Television and Video Almanac,* there were 742,400,000 prerecorded videocassettes sold in the United States in 1999 and 4,100,000 DVDs shipped to dealers in 2001.[17]

THE LIBRARY OF TOMORROW

Given the facts of publishing, the demand by library users for great numbers of all media, and the pressures on library budgets imposed by the actual and perceived demand for electronic documents and resources, it is easy to see that libraries are being pulled in opposing directions. As ever, we come back to budgets and the priorities they embody. Unfortunately, most libraries have limited materials budgets in which an increase in expenditure in one area must be balanced by decreases in others. Though most expenditures for access to electronic resources are, in reality, materials expenditures—the acquisition of, or acquisition of access to, electronic resources—there are also expenditures for the infrastructure that surrounds those acquisitions. Books, serials, maps, and scores once processed, take up space and need shelving and other storage devices. In a similar fashion, electronic resources mandate not only the terminals that library workers and library users need but also a physical infrastructure (wiring, servers, wireless networks, LANs) and, even more expensive and continuing, a human infrastructure of programmers, technicians, system analysts, and the like. The latter, once in place, form a powerful special interest lobby for even more expenditures in new technology (let us not forget that innovation in computer technology is a matter of months, or even weeks).

A library systems department is staffed by experts who are usually paid more than their peers in the rest of the library and are masters of the mysteries that interest library staff, library users, and controllers of the library's purse strings the most. Once a library has such a department, it must live with the fact that this group has enormous influence, passive and active, over the library's planning and budgeting processes. Compound that with a zeitgeist which uncritically endorses the popular media perception of libraries and the "information revolution," and you have an almost irresistible force that drains money from all other areas of the library to feed the insatiable appetites of the "information technology" lobby.[18]

It behooves all of us with responsibilities for libraries and their budgets to resist these strong forces and to seek balance in the expenditures and attention devoted to different kinds of library materials. If you believe that libraries are going to change utterly or vanish from the face of the earth, seeking such balance must seem quixotic. If you believe, as I do, that libraries are going through an interesting period in their evolution (different in degree but not in kind from previous periods) and that we must ensure that all materials are adequately represented in our libraries, then balance and harmony are essential. The selector and the collection developer alike must be keenly aware of each medium in which the library collects (or subscribes) and must balance the strengths and limitations of each against the others.

THE DIGITAL DIVIDE

All clichés are true to some extent, and the "digital divide"—the great cliché of the "information age" (a cliché within a cliché)—is as true as any other. The notion is that if you are white, well-off, suburban, able-bodied, middle-aged, etc., you will be more likely to have ready access to the Internet than someone who is a member of a minority, poor, young, old, disabled, or who lives in a rural area or an inner city. Of course, anyone could name fifty things of greater or lesser importance than access to the Internet that are more likely to be accessible to the former group or, for that matter, to someone who is American, Canadian, western European, Japanese, or Australian as opposed to someone living outside those countries and regions.

There are a number of governmental bodies (at various levels) and private-sector groups that have dedicated themselves to reducing the digital divide. An example of the latter—DigitalDivide—is a collaborative effort between Harvard University and MIT aimed at reducing the gap "between those able to benefit by digital technologies and those who are not."[19] They regard this as the new battleground in world affairs and propose extensive and expensive national and international strategies. In February 2002, the U.S. Department of Commerce released *A Nation Online,* an extensive survey (based on census figures) of the use of the Internet by Americans.[20] Though the survey trumpets the number of people who have Internet access, it also discusses what it calls, spookily, "The Unconnected." As of September 2001, these poor souls comprised 46.1 percent of persons and 49.5 percent of households. These people are disproportionately poor, have lower levels of education, are often African-American or Hispanic, or are disabled. The report is sanguine about the future because of the growth rates in Internet access that it describes, but offers no overall solution to the divide it details with such care.

The digital divide within developed countries and between developed countries and the Third World is real, of course. It depends mostly on money and power. Those with both have all the Internet access they wish. Those without either have limited or no access. This is also true, in the United States, with regard to access to health care, quality education, readily available transportation, and a host of other services. Crucially to this discussion, it also holds true for access to library services in general. Efforts aimed at bridging the digital divide without making any other changes are the twenty-first-century equivalents of Victorian charity, which sought to solve only one aspect of the multidimensional handicaps under which the poor then labored. Warm clothes for the "deserving poor" are all very well but don't do much good if those poor live in areas where a lack of sanitation leads to periodic outbreaks of cholera. Many of today's poor and otherwise disadvantaged do suffer from a lack of access to the kind of information that can be found readily on the Internet, but they also suffer from underfunded public education, economically straitened libraries, low levels of literacy, and a debased culture of lowbrow entertainment. How are people living in such a culture going to have their lives and mental landscapes changed by being given access to the Internet?

Fresno County lies in the heart of California's great Central Valley—the richest agricultural land in the world. There are many wealthy people in the county and its eponymous city, but the county has a 14- or 15-percent unemployment rate even in the best of times. This is because it is home, for at least part of the year, to large numbers of seasonal and migrant farm workers. The overwhelming majority of these workers are Mexican or Mexican-American. Poverty, ill health, low levels of literacy, inadequate housing, and encounters with prejudice (based on appearance and language) are the common coin of their lives. Their children (who may be the only bilingual members of the family) attend poor schools that have the worst school libraries in the United States. The figures for school libraries statewide in California are dismal, but you can rest assured that those for the Central Valley are worse. A report put out by the state's Department of Education makes the following points:

> The Internet does not replace the need for books and often increases the demand for up-to-date library materials.

> Seven out of eight schools in California do *not* have professional library staffing for half a day or more. While the national ratio of library media specialist to students is 1:882, the California ratio, K–12, is 1:5,342.[21]

The picture is clear. Let us take a K–12 student in Parlier, Orange Cove, or Mendota (all rural communities in Fresno County) for whom English is a second language and who lives with her large family in the kind of substandard housing typically occupied by her socioeconomic group. The chances are that her school is underfunded, there is no librarian in her school library, and the books available in that library are fewer and older than in a school library in any other state. The local public library is open from 10:30 to 6 on Monday to Thursday and 10 to 2 on Saturday and is closed on Fridays and Sundays. How will access to the Internet improve this student's mental life and her chances for success in life? Just ponder the facts that only 40 percent of first-year students admitted to California State University are proficient in mathematics, only 47 percent are proficient in English, and those admissions are the top 30 percent of high school graduates.[22] Does anyone think this grim picture would be much brighter if there were universal access to the Internet and all the other objective circumstances remained the same?

There is a divide, one that is far greater than the digital divide, of longer standing, and of far more import, but it is a societal divide—one that discriminates against minorities and the poor in terms of education, health care, housing, employment opportunities, literacy, and all the other factors that are vital to learning, empowerment, and the pursuit of happiness. Libraries play an important part in bridging that divide, but we should not fool ourselves into thinking that it can be bridged, or even significantly narrowed, by wiring every library and classroom for Internet access. Spending money on encouraging reading; providing each child with plenty of new, readily accessible books in her school library and in the children's departments of public libraries (with user-friendly hours); and ensuring every child the services of dedicated, well-compensated librarians would do far more to help than any amount of wiring. Not enough money? In that case, where is the money to come from to support the promiscuous expansion of Internet access? The latter goes well beyond wiring and encompasses the provision of technicians and information-competence instructors; the replacement of hardware and software every year or so; and all the other elements of a massive technological and human infrastructure needed to address only one element, and not the most important element, of the divide that threatens our society.

NOTES

1. Deyan Sudjic, "Keep It Quiet, This Is a Library," *The Observer Review,* November 18, 2001, 10.

2. Peter Brophy, "Strategic Issues for Academic Libraries," *Relay: The Journal of the UC&R,* no. 52 (2002): 4–5.

3. I was most recently the object of such accusations made by John Berry (the *Library Journal* editor) in a review of my book *Our Enduring Strengths* in *College & Research Libraries,* January 2002.

4. William Y. Arms, "Automated Digital Libraries: How Effectively Can Computers Be Used for the Skilled Tasks of Professional Librarianship?" *D-Lib Magazine,* July 2000. Page numbers are given in parentheses in my quotations of this article.

5. William Y. Arms, *Digital Libraries* (Boston: MIT Press, 2001).

6. William Y. Arms, "Relaxing Assumptions about the Future of Digital Libraries: The Hare and the Tortoise," *D-Lib Magazine,* April 1997, 2.

7. Arms, "Relaxing Assumptions," 2.

8. Carol Peterson, Elizabeth Cowell, and Jim Jacobs, "Government Documents at the Crossroads," *American Libraries,* September 2001, 52–55.

9. All statistics are from *The Bowker Annual,* 46th ed. (Reed Elsevier, 2001).

10. OCLC website, at http://www.oclc.org/western/news/sep01/sep01_worldcat_stats_cts.htm.

11. Ibid.

12. *Standard Periodical Directory,* 24th ed. (New York: Oxbridge Communications, 2001).

13. Cited at www.magazine.org/resources/fact-sheets.

14. *Ulrich's* website, at www.ulrichsweb.com.

15. See www.riaa.org/MD-US-6,cfm.

16. Chris Morris, column in *Billboard,* May 12, 2001.

17. *International Video and Television Almanac, 2001* (Larchmont, N.Y.: Quigley, 2001).

18. See, among the thousands like it, a staggeringly clichéd article by Tanya Schevitz called "A New Chapter for Libraries," *San Francisco Chronicle,* February 10, 2002, p. A1.

19. DigitalDivide website, at www.digitaldivide.org/over.html.

20. U.S. Department of Commerce, *A Nation Online: How Americans Are Expanding Their Use of the Internet* (Washington, D.C.: Government Printing Office, 2002).

21. California Department of Education, *A Statistical Snapshot of California School Libraries,* available at www.cde.ca.gov/cilbranch/eltdiv/library/statis.html.

22. California State University, Chancellor's Office, report issued on January 23, 2002.

4 Reading in a Digital World

literate: 1a. characterized by or possessed of learning . . .
1b. able to read and write . . . [1]

VERY FEW PEOPLE ARE OVERTLY AGAINST LITERACY THESE DAYS. VICTORIAN TORIES SAW mass literacy as a threat to the established order—as indeed, it was—but even their modern counterparts dare not utter such thoughts. The general embrace of literacy is due largely to the fact that the term encompasses so much and is so vague in application. It is clear from popular and scholarly writings on the topic and from the many pronouncements of politicians and educators that there is no widely accepted definition of "literacy." Since any fruitful discussion must proceed on the basis of a shared vocabulary, it is important to precede the argument by defining the word "literacy" and the various phrases that contain it. (In this context, commonly used phrases such as "computer literacy" and "visual literacy" verge on the meaningless at best and are actively dangerous when they carry an implied equality with real literacy or, worse, are seen as a substitute for it.)

As can be seen from the definitions in *Webster's Third New International Dictionary* given in the epigraph, there are two, in some sense antithetical, official definitions of literacy ("the state of being literate," as defined in *Webster's*). In its most basic definition, the word is concerned with the simple ability to read and write *at some level.* If one sticks to that narrow definition, a second-grader who can read and write is literate and so is Harold Bloom.[2] Clearly there is greater depth to a more expansive definition of "literacy" (the one that is concerned with learning)—one that goes far beyond the elementary ability to read and write. What I mean by "literacy" (or "full literacy") is the lifelong process of learning to read and write ever more deeply and effectively after one has mastered the mechanics of reading and writing. These latter activities are mutually interdependent. One cannot write well if one cannot read well, and the more capable a person is of the sustained reading of complex texts, the more likely he or she is to be able to express complex thoughts in writing. When employers and university teachers complain of the inability of college students and graduates to write correctly in clear declarative English, they are really complaining about the fact that these young people are not in the habit of reading. This is not the fault of the students, however. Any system that takes the best and brightest and fails to inculcate the habit and the love of reading in them is a comprehensive and expensive failure.

The great thing for the child of today is to form the habit of reading so that they [*sic*] may escape sometimes from their surroundings into different ages and different moods.

— Eleanor Roosevelt[3]

"Functional literacy" is the ability to read and write at a level that will enable someone to live a normal exterior life (though they are likely to have a shrunken interior life). The ability to do such things as read an article in a tabloid newspaper, fill out an application form, and follow directions to another place is essential to modern life. If you cannot read warning signs and traffic directions your life may be in danger. If you cannot fill out an application form, most jobs are closed to you. Though there are millions of Americans who cannot do these things (the "illiterate"), there are millions more who can (the "functionally literate") but who cannot read a book, follow a lengthy article in the *Los Angeles Times,* or write a persuasive letter. Then there are those who can do such things but choose not to (the "aliterate"). In their lives they read what they must but no more and write, if at all, using debased forms such as "text messaging." There is another useful term that is not much used today—the "technically literate." These are people who can read aloud from a simple text or write a letter containing simple words only. They can read and write, but much of what they read means little to them, and they write using simple words because those are the only ones they understand. In common usage, all of these types, with the exception of the illiterate, would be described as "literate," but clearly such a description is so broad as to be useless in any serious discussion. What we cannot overemphasize is the importance of reading to the development of the mind and the processes of education and lifelong learning.

On December 27, 2001, during the mid-holiday lull, I listened to National Public Radio's two-hour program *Morning Edition*. One eight- to ten-minute section consisted of an interview with Harold Bloom and readings from his anthology intended for "extremely intelligent children of all ages."[4] Another section dealt with the inventor and marketer of a process for audiovisual materials on the Web. A third section dealt with the threats to local schools from the slowing economy and consequent cuts in state funding. All dealt, with varying degrees of directness, with the importance of reading in today's society.

Bloom, of course, is concerned with the lower levels of literacy he encounters nowadays as compared with two or three decades ago—a decline that is especially worrying since the people he deals with every day are students at Yale University and could be expected to be the crème de la crème. He has famously denounced the *Harry Potter* books for their "clichéd writing" and "banal middle class sensibility" and offers an anthology of readings from the Western (largely nineteenth-century) canon that enlarge the imagination and enrich the life of the mind.

The web mogul on the radio program mentioned many applications of his "streaming audio and video" system. These included a "celestial jukebox" and global, instantaneous access to any desired film or video via the Web. He explicitly stated that people nowadays prefer listening and watching to reading. This may well be true regarding the amusements and diversions to which his RealPlayer system is dedicated and is almost certainly true in terms of numbers. The reader will notice that the web mogul, unlike Bloom, offers no value judgments on the relative quality of what is listened to, watched, or read, and still less as to the superior intellectual quality of the reading experience. To Bloom, reading is a cultural experience of the highest importance to the development of the human mind and the betterment of society as a whole. Furthermore, he places great importance on *what* is read as well as on reading itself. In short, he is a cultural elitist with no fear of making value judgments. To the streaming audio/video man, watching a Seattle Mariners' game, listening to a "rap artist," and reading a novel by John Updike are all the same. The wonders of the technology that gives us a "celestial jukebox" and similar audiovisual diversions are all that matters to him—his concerns are with process, not content.

What do the teachers and school administrators of the third section have to do with the implicit conflict between Bloom and his polar opposite? Their ten minutes were taken up with the effects of the 2001 recession on such matters as test scores, remedial and special education in disadvantaged areas, and technology (computers) in the classroom. The test scores, of course, are concerned with reading and other skills and textbooks are among the things affected by the budget cuts, but nowhere in the piece was any aspect of literacy other than the ability to read at grade level mentioned. It seems that apart from a few people like Bloom who are easily stereotyped as "elitists" or "reactionaries," literacy has either ceased to be a matter of concern or is regarded as something that concerns, and only concerns, the mechanics of the reading process. This is by no means a modern issue only. In a celebrated jeremiad published in 1933, Professor H. R. Huse discussed the "illiteracy of the literate."[5] He described an educational system in which pupils could read and pronounce words but were incapable of understanding them. He attempted to show "the limitations of a merely technical literacy, why it is that, instead of a body of intelligent citizens rising to the pride and dignity of independent minds, we have the familiar suggestible masses fed on the daily bread of 'hokum,' conditioned, manipulated at will."[6] All that was well before the advent of television and the Internet.

On the same day that the National Public Radio program aired, my local newspaper ran a story on a local teacher of literacy in an elementary school.[7] Though again focused on process, this article had something important to say about literacy—something that is often taken for granted, or is the object of lip service, or is simply ignored. "It [the teaching of reading and writing] is all aimed at one basic goal. Making sure that students get a solid foundation in literacy, *the principal underpinning of career success and personal achievement*" (emphasis added). Harold Bloom might quarrel with putting "career success" first, but surely not with the notion that reading and writing are the principal underpinning of personal development and success in life. It is possible to achieve material success and even, as we now know, to achieve high office while being semiliterate. But it is absolutely impossible to be a fully realized human being and to understand the heights and depths of the human condition without developed literacy.

In spite of my earnestness, I found reading a pleasurable activity. I came to enjoy the lonely good company of books. Early on weekday mornings, I'd read in my bed. I'd feel a mysterious comfort then, reading in the quiet dawn—the blue-gray silence interrupted by the occasional churning of the refrigerator motor a few rooms away or the more distant sounds of a city bus beginning its run. On weekends I'd go to the public library to read, surrounded by old men and women. Or, if the weather were fine, I would take my books to the park and read in the shade of a tree.

—Richard Rodriguez[8]

As a pupil, he had learned to read, write, and figure through the rule of three. To be able to write well at ten years of age was an accomplishment of distinction, and in this art Abraham excelled. His stepmother stated that he was "diligent for knowledge, wished to know, and if pains and labor would get it was sure to get it." He did not advance through the accepted channels of higher education as he "was never in a college or Academy as a student." He followed a program of reading and study that he set up for himself, and his self-imposed discipline was rigid. His desire to know, to understand, was unquenchable.

—Louis A. Warren[9]

Professor Huse complained of the distractions of large-circulation periodicals and quoted Alben Barkley (writing in *The New Republic* in 1929) on the topic. "A wood-pulp magazine is one of the most diluted forms of pabulum obtainable in America. It is just a half-rung below the average Hollywood movie. For that reason, it is aside from the newspaper, the favorite reading matter of a huge proportion of the reading public."[10] A modern observer might comment that at least they were reading something, but the point being made was that such low-level reading did not give readers an extended vocabulary of understood words and, therefore, left them incapable of reading at a higher level.

The menace (if it was that) of the wood pulps was as nothing compared with the forces that pull people away from full literacy today. In place of the cinema showing one film a week and cheap magazines, we have 21-screen cineplexes, more magazines than the wood pulps ever dreamed of, 200-channel television, cell phones, electronic and digital games, home entertainment centers, DVDs, CDs, and the Internet and the Web. We have democratized entertainment, and the tide running against literacy seventy years ago is now a tsunami resistible only by those who have had reading instilled in them from their earliest years. The love of reading is a hardy and tenacious plant, but its seeds must be planted early and nourished into maturity. I believe that libraries have an important and necessary role in nourishing and encouraging literacy. I also believe that many libraries have failed to play that role to the fullest extent possible.

The American Library Association maintains an Office for Literacy and Outreach Services (OLOS). This body, which undoubtedly does much good work, is focused largely at the "threshold" literacy problem I alluded to earlier. Through highly publicized and generously funded initiatives such as Literacy in Libraries across America (a joint project of the ALA and the Lila Wallace–

Reader's Digest Fund), the "action area" 21st Century Literacy, and the website www.Buildliteracy.org, the OLOS provides advice and resources to help use public libraries as centers for teaching adults to read and improve their reading skills. At the OLOS website one finds the following interesting statements:

> Literacy has been a focus of the American Library Association throughout its 125-year history. 21st Century Literacy is one of five key action areas adopted by the American Library Association to fulfill its mission of providing the highest quality library and information services for all people. Helping children and adults develop skills they need to fully participate in an information society—whether it's learning to read or exploring the Internet—is central to that mission.
>
> The American Library Association has worked in a variety of ways to expand the vision of what it means to be literate in a global information society. Activities include the promotion of reading, literacy education for librarians, and the development of model programs. The association has well-established channels for mobilizing library supporters and has been instrumental in encouraging federal funding for literacy efforts. The association also works with national leaders to support literacy programs.

The emphasis is not on literacy as a means of improving the mind and providing education over a lifetime, but on the much more utilitarian development of skills adults and children "need to fully participate in an information society—whether it's learning to read or exploring the Internet." Literacy is reduced to the ability to read and write and, equally, to exploring the Internet. However much the latter may matter to living in "an information society," it cannot reasonably be assigned the importance of the sustained reading or writing of complex texts. The truth is, I suspect, that utilitarian principles embrace the whole concept of literacy as promoted by the OLOS and its programs. In this view, one should learn to read and write in order to be able to function in an increasingly postliterate society. Just as "exploring the Internet" is deemed important, so is reading a simple set of instructions, deciphering the facts found in a reference source, and filling out simple forms. The joy of reading, its capacity to improve and delight, do not lie within the purview of this earnest desire to equip people for a life of work and entertainment in a trivially utilitarian society. I believe the ALA would be far more effective in promoting literacy if it were to pursue the deeper

---

Are there not some pursuits we practice because they are good in themselves, and some pleasures that are final? And is this [reading] not among them?

—Virginia Woolf[11]

issues—those that go far beyond the mere ability to read and write and even farther beyond the ability to use the Internet. The latter, in fact, supports my case. Any fool can find *something* on the Internet—the important thing is the ability to choose relevant sources and assess whatever it is one finds. This ability ("critical thinking") is what information-competence teachers seek to inculcate. Why then do literacy teachers content themselves with the mechanics of reading and writing and not the uses to which those mechanics can be put?

A CULTURAL DIVIDE

What should librarians do to promote true literacy that goes beyond the mechanics of reading and writing? This question goes to the heart of the often-unspoken great divide in the profession of librarianship. That divide is often, though not always, generational. It involves a deeper issue than the usual divides between library educators and practitioners; and between information scientists and the library profession. It rests on the division between the people of the book and the people of the byte. This is a simplistic dichotomy, because many of the former are very keen on the use of computers when appropriate and at least some of the latter are great readers, but it does delineate the two tendencies. The people of the book are often seen as being opponents of the byte, resisting the inevitable as their "outmoded form of communication" is cast on the ash heap of history. In turn, they often see the people of the byte as vandals and technophiliacs who are indifferent to learning and culture. Most people see these as the stereotypes they are, but in doing so, they ignore the fact that the dichotomy is real; the lack of understanding between the (mostly older) people of the book and the (mostly younger) people of the byte is a threat to the future of the library profession.

Lawrence Clark Powell wrote:

> As long as books are with us—and I see no end of books in libraries, *as the basic stuff of librarians,* no matter what supplementary media are present—as long as books are basic, the good librarian will maintain physical contact with books, handling them for himself and for others [emphasis added].[12]

To some, these thirty-year-old words will seem as if from a century ago. Only a person of the book can understand the tactility that is an essential part of the world of the reader and, still more, the idea that books are, and will remain, the basic stuff of the librarian's work. The very idea of sustained reading for instruction and pleasure must verge on the quaint to someone who believes that "information competence" is solely a matter of navigating the Web and finding something of value therein. Powell goes on to write in the same lecture:

> librarianship is a learned profession, calling for intellectual skill . . . .
> Knowledge is truly power. As librarians we have close and constant access to
> the world's knowledge . . . we must also penetrate the covers of books to the
> contents. We must know what it is that readers seek and where to find it. How
> do we gain such varied knowledge? By lifelong learning, by reading and study
> that begins when we are young and in school, *and that never ends,* if we are to
> become good, powerful, useful librarians. The good librarian is a reservoir of
> knowledge, a well of learning, a fountain of culture [emphasis added].[13]

There must be many modern librarians—people of the byte—who would find such sentiments eccentric at best and vainglorious and overweening at worst. It is true that few of us can be a Lawrence Clark Powell—scholar, librarian, writer, educator, and philosopher—but we can and should be able to aspire to his ideals. After all, few of us are latter-day Ranganathans or Deweys, either, but that does not stop us trying to catalogue well. I would dare to suggest that, more than thirty years after Powell spoke, the world of libraries would be a better place if more librarians strove for the ideal of lifelong learning through serious reading that he recommended. Recorded knowledge is to be found in books and other printed texts and not, generally speaking, on the Internet. Recorded knowledge is not easy to absorb even in the few cases in which it is found in the latter. The use of "e-books" (itself a revealing term) is concentrated on manuals, reference works, and other texts from which snippets may be extracted and used out of their context. There is, it appears, only a small hobbyist or cult market for even the lowest form of literature on the Web.

In response, the people of the byte will say, as they have been saying for many years, that we are in a transitional phase. Their line is that just as the horse-drawn vehicle was slow to give way to the horseless carriage and the scroll to the codex, the book is doomed to a lingering death at the hands of the computer. Analogies are to thinking what quicksands are to beach walking, and when the careful reader reads of the passing of the buggy whip industry, she is careful to ignore the facile and fatal charms of the common analogy. Such arguments and would-be parallels are sometimes advanced for negative reasons. We should not forget that some people of the byte are not at all interested in the book and the traditions of learning, authenticity, and civilization it embodies. Take, for example, James J. O'Donnell, a classicist turned university administrator who has won some minor acclaim by airing his contrarian views to, among others, librarians.

Perhaps one way to make that self-awareness easier is to make ourselves deliberately more conscious of the unnaturalness of this whole affair our culture has with books. We long ago ceased to see the oddity of textuality and its institutions—publishers who produce books, libraries who treasure and make them available, scholars who pass along the mystic arts of interpretation to students. Is it not strange that we take the spoken word, the most insubstantial of human creations, and try, through textuality, to freeze it forever; and again, to give the frozen words of those who are dead and gone, or at least far absent, control over our own experience of the lived here and now? . . . . I have very little business caring for the future of the book. Books are only secondary bearers of culture. "Western civilization" (or whatever other allegorical creature we cook up to embody our self esteem) is not something to be cherished.[14]

All this from someone who claims in the same passage to have "passion and affection" for books! One hardly knows where to begin. Is not the whole point of what O'Donnell dismisses as "Western civilization" that we allow the "frozen words" of the dead to influence and inspire our life here and now? Is not the alternative a reversion to a savage state of experiencing the present and fearing the future because we have no collective memory to guide us? What would our lives be like if we lacked access to the frozen words of Darwin and Shakespeare, Lincoln and Martin Luther King Jr.? Perhaps I am being duped and O'Donnell is a brilliant satirist of the fatuities of deconstructionists. I suppose that is possible, but if so, it must be a brilliantly sustained hoax, since O'Donnell has written and spoken in the same vein many times. Let us assume he is serious and really means to criticize "textuality" as an aberration in human history. It may well prove to have been an aberration and we may be reduced by the death of the book to a state feared by another contributor to the symposium at which O'Donnell spoke:

> What will happen, then, when children (and adults) find introducing a three-dimensional video of, say, a rhinoceros, into a discussion so easy that they increasingly lose the ability to formulate abstract or physical descriptions? McLuhan has persuasively argued that written language had to exist before logical, causal thinking could become so widespread. If so, what will happen when we increasingly abandon alphanumeric text, when we would truly find ourselves beyond the book?[15]

These questions go to the heart of the problem. If we are to preserve our culture, we need both the frozen words in books and other texts and we need people who can interact with those frozen words in a complex and sustained manner. In short, we need books and lifelong learning and true literacy if we are not to regress to a state of sensation and the manifold distortions of the oral tradition. It may be that O'Donnell and his ilk would prefer to exist in a world of myth and dimly apprehended reality—an ahistorical world of shadows and ignorance (a very odd stance for a classicist), but I stand with those who cherish the stability, authenticity, and fixity of the frozen word and the onward transmittal of the human record.

THE ROLE OF THE LIBRARIAN IN TRUE LITERACY

Though I believe that libraries have a great and continuing role in spreading functional literacy (the ability to read and write well enough to navigate modern society), I also believe they have an even more important role in the encouragement and support of true literacy (enabling people to become learned through reading). The first and probably most important action is to supply library users with a substantial and constantly refreshed collection of books on a variety of topics of interest. The reduction of some public library collections to modern best-sellers, popular magazines, videos and the like is simply insufficient to foster reading and literacy in the communities they serve. Almost as important are the provision of good children's library collections, trained and dedicated children's librarians, and a wide range of programs to foster reading and the love of literature from an early age. If children are regular visitors to a local public library and have good school library services, they not only learn to read earlier but also learn to love reading—a love that will sustain them throughout their lives.

Following the excellent example of the Library of Congress's Center for the Book, and the parallel centers in forty-seven states, libraries of all kinds should have a continuing program of events, displays, clubs, discussions, and lectures aimed at promoting and encouraging reading. Children's libraries are well placed to organize events around storytelling and reading competitions. Similarly, school libraries should work with teachers to integrate reading into all aspects of the K–12 curriculum and encourage students to use a wide variety of printed sources in their research and studies. Encouraging young children to rely on the Internet as the sole or primary source of data and information for their studies is little short of a betrayal. Diverting them from such reliance into the path of sustained reading as a means of acquiring knowledge is a sacred duty for both children's and school librarians. They can and should use all the methods at their disposal to carry out that duty. Public libraries are ideally situated to make literacy-related efforts an important and visible part of the life of their communities.

A spectacular example of a literacy campaign in which public libraries play a pivotal role is the idea that whole communities can come together in reading one book at the same time. Such a project was first tried in Seattle in 1998 with Harper Lee's *To Kill a Mockingbird*. The city of Chicago (with the enthusiastic support of Mayor Richard Daley) took up the idea in the fall of 2001. The California Council of the Humanities is recommending that all Californians read John Steinbeck's *The Grapes of Wrath* as part of a project called "My story is California's story." Other towns and cities are expected to follow suit. It would be very easy to criticize such efforts as tokenish and the choice of reading as "safe" and irretrievably middlebrow, but that would, in my opinion, be missing the point. In isolation, such projects might be futile, but as visible and news-worthy examples of a commitment to literacy and shared experience they are invaluable. Just imagine, for example, the effect on California's life if everyone living there actually read and discussed *The Grapes of Wrath*. At a minimum, there would be a far greater understanding of one of the events—the Depression-era migration from the Dust Bowl to the Golden State—that helped shape modern California. Beyond that, there would be an understanding of the similarities between the treatment of the "Okies" in the 1930s and the treatment of Mexican and Southeast Asian farm workers today. This would induce a sense of community and an understanding of a complex and diverse state. Beyond even that, many who read Steinbeck's book as their first book in years would have their eyes opened to the joy and value of reading—something that could well change their lives.

Some special libraries are so rooted in technology that their involvement in books is necessarily limited. Others have major print collections and can at least cooperate with other libraries and with their communities in promoting literacy. Academic libraries of all kinds and sizes have a most important role to play in advancing true literacy. Not only should they maintain good print collections and engage in all the events, programs, displays, and lectures that they can, but they must work with teaching faculty and campus administrators to ensure that reading is a central part of the curriculum. Many have criticized the "great books" approach on the grounds of elitism and ethnocentrism, but such pro-grams, in the modern world, need not suffer from either flaw. Is it elitist to promote and reward sustained reading? Is it ethnocentric to identify and promote the greatest products of the human spirit written by men and women from all cultures, countries, and times? The writings of "dead white males" have much to offer, but so do the writings of women and those of people of color and from other countries and cultures. University and college curricula should be centered on the reading of all the best texts that the world has to offer and should recognize that an educated person must possess knowledge of those texts and the skills necessary to profit from them. Academic librarianship cannot afford to ignore these truths or to remain passive at a time when the active promotion of reading and literacy is vital to the future of the academy and society.

NOTES

1. *Webster's Third New International Dictionary of the English Language* (Springfield, Mass.: G&C Merriam, 1976), 1321.

2. Harold Bloom is an author and Yale professor famous for his emphasis on the value of reading.

3. Eleanor Roosevelt to Henry Canby, letter of November 6, 1929, quoted in Blanche Wiesen Cook, *Eleanor Roosevelt* (New York: Viking, 1992), 1:514–15.

4. Harold Bloom, ed., *Stories and Poems for Extremely Intelligent Children of All Ages* (New York: Scribner, 2001).

5. H. R. Huse, *The Illiteracy of the Literate* (New York: D. Appleton-Century, 1933).

6. Huse, *Illiteracy*, vi.

7. Russell Minick, "Teaching Center Stage: All-Star Teacher, Jaymee Harris," *Fresno Bee,* December 27, 2001, p. B7.

8. Richard Rodriguez, *Hunger of Memory* (New York: Bantam, 1983), 62–63.

9. Louis A. Warren, *Lincoln's Youth: Indiana Years, Seven to Twenty-One, 1816–1830* (Westport, Conn.: Greenwood, reprinted 1976), 210–11.

10. Huse, *Illiteracy*, 6.

11. Virginia Woolf, "How Should One Read a Book," in *The Common Reader: Second Series* (London: Hogarth, 1932).

12. Lawrence Clark Powell, *The Three Hs* (Los Angeles: Press in the Gatehouse, 1971), 2.

13. Powell, *Three Hs*, 5.

14. James J. O'Donnell, "Trimethius, McLuhan, Cassiodorus," in *The Future of the Book*, ed. Geoffrey Nunberg (Berkeley: University of California Press, 1996), 54.

15. George P. Landow, "Twenty Minutes into the Future," in *Future of the Book*, 234.

5   The Nature of the Web

UNTIL THE LAST THIRD OF THE NINETEENTH CENTURY, GEOGRAPHERS CREATED MAPS OF the world and of "newly discovered" regions that were a mixture of reasonably accurate graphic data about charted areas and wild guesses and fantasies about uncharted ones. These early maps showed the various *terrae incognitae,* invented islands and continents, and uncharted seas to be populated with dragons, three-headed men, krakens, hippogriffs, anthropophagi, and other fabulous creatures. As late Victorian and twentieth-century explorers and mapmakers charted more of the land and oceans, such fantastic embellishments gave way to the factual depiction of real places, rivers, islands, etc. It seems to me that we are in the position of those early cartographers with respect to the Web. It is a fantastic world of which we know only some of the borders and the well-settled parts of the interior. People have even written extensively of the "invisible Web"—a term that rivals any in medieval cosmology.[1] We need to create accurate maps of the Web, both visible and "invisible." Beyond that, we must enumerate its content and provide an adequate taxonomy for it. When we have those three things—accurate maps, counts, and a taxonomy—we will be prepared to integrate the Web fully into library services.

The World Wide Web is a paradoxical, often counterintuitive presence in individual societies and in the global electronic connectivity—cyberspace—that is usurping many of the individual attributes of those societies. It is already ubiquitous in the life of the middle and upper classes in the developed world and the affluent in the developing world. The Web is as much a part of globalization as the multinational corporations who use and abuse it every day and the various free-trade agreements between nations and continental blocs. It is both global and personal, a means of communication between all the people of the world and between the members of tiny, obsessive cliques that like to call themselves "communities." It is a practical engine that delivers books, socks, gardening tools, and handmade candles at the touch of a keyboard. It is also a mythical presence—an infinite electronic hall of mirrors in which the thoughts and prejudices of millions carom, shift shape, and reverberate for nanoseconds, years, or periods in between.

THE ROLE OF THE WEB AND ITS PROBLEMS

It is hard to believe that the first web page in North America was created at Stanford University as recently as November 1991. In not much more than a decade, the World Wide Web has become a central part of communications and commerce, nationally and internationally. (It should be noted that although direct selling on the Web only accounted for 3–5 percent of all selling in 2002, the Web facilitates commerce in many more ways indirectly.) The Web's rise and spread has been so dramatic that it is seen by some hyperventilators as the Second Coming of Gutenberg—the essential infrastructure of a new age aborning.

One does not have to be a true believer to acknowledge that the Web is a remarkable achievement, and like all great innovations as much a leap of the human imagination as a technological feat. The Web has brought us much and will, when the dust settles, be seen as a major advance in communications technology. However, it has, as I write, two major problems. The first is that the Web has metastasized to an almost ungraspable size, and this has led to a level of disorganization at which precision and recall in searching are impossible dreams— I shall address this in detail in later chapters. The second problem is that the Web includes some of the heights and almost all of the depths of human nature. For every major achievement of humanity that the Web has made possible, such as the Library of Congress's American Memory Project, there are thousands of manifestations of greed, prurience, lunacy, violence, vacuity, and crassness. All forms of human communication have been used for such dross—one need only think of "penny dreadfuls," tabloid newspapers, "gangsta rap" recordings, Jean-Claude Van Damme movies, "reality" television programs, and "easy listening" radio—but none on this scale. Depending on one's sensibilities, one can see the lack of control and the lack of filtering on the Web as a fine thing or as a cultural disaster. But no one, whether libertarian or elitist, utopian or aesthete, can deny the fact that the Web contains much that is worthless, meretricious, and vulgar. Moreover, it also contains much that is none of these things but that is of transient value, local value, or no value at all to anyone but that material's creator.

If the Web is to be integrated fully into library services, we must find some way of coming to terms with these facts. In particular, it is difficult for a profession that espouses tolerance and intellectual freedom as core values to reach an accommodation with what could be seen as censorship. S. R. Ranganathan observed that "bad thought laid bare to the world is rendered sterile." This is a plausible argument when deciding whether it should be legal to publish, say, *Mein Kampf* or *The Protocols of the Elders of Zion*.[2] Ranganathan's aphorism can also be useful when considering whether there should be attempts to close down particular websites—for example, the racist, Holocaust revisionist, and other antisocial sites that exist in great profusion. The arguments against such action include those based on the immorality of censorship and in defense of intellectual freedom, but as is the case with combating the sex-obsessed "filterers," the most cogent argument is that of practicality. Just as it seems futile to argue whether filtering is a good thing, since only the closed-minded are unable to see that filtering does not work, both high-minded and base attempts to censor the Web run up against the near-impossibility of doing so in a democratic society. Even in nondemocratic societies, the only effective way to censor the Web seems to be to severely limit access to computers, as the current Chinese government is finding out the hard way.

When it comes to using the Web in libraries there is, as is the case with "traditional" publications, a huge difference between censorship and discrimination (in the non-pejorative sense). Almost all librarians are in favor of anyone publishing whatever he or she wishes, but that predilection does not oblige any library to acquire that publication. The process is known as "selection" and consists of making judgments—exercising discrimination—about what fits best with the mission of the library, what is valuable or of less value, and what is worthwhile and what is not. Publishers play an important role in selecting and editing authors' manuscripts, composers' and performers' productions, etc. To a lesser extent, booksellers and other vendors also influence the size and nature of the market for library materials. Because of their efforts, the universe of "traditional" materials from which items are selected for the library is far smaller and far more coherent than that of the Web. The same principles apply in using the Web, however, despite the fact that the scale and degree of muddle are far greater.

WHAT IS A "DOCUMENT"?

Before we proceed to an examination of the contents of the Web, we need to consider a topic that has hitherto been the province of learned and somewhat rarefied discussion. We need to pose the question examined by the last of the great documentalists, Michael Buckland: What is a document?[3] This is a crucial question because it lies at the heart of the definition of the province of libraries—recorded knowledge (including literary works) and information, the important word being "recorded." Libraries are not concerned with knowledge and information in general—these have to be recorded in words, images, sounds, or symbols before they can form a part of library collections, services, and programs. In the distant, more manageable past we thought of a document as a text—printed or written—with a beginning, middle, and end. This coherent, easily graspable concept has been fraying at the edges for a century at least. Photographs are documents, whether accompanied by text or not. So are sound recordings, filmstrips, moving pictures, and video recordings. All these have been created by one or more people in a conscious attempt to record thoughts, images, sounds, and symbols.

What, however, are we to make of an object—for example, an animal—as document? This possibility was raised by Suzanne Briet when she argued that an antelope running wild in Africa is not a document, but the same animal captured, taken to a zoo, and used as the object of study is.[4] Buckland summarizes her line of thinking as being, essentially, that a document must be a physical object, intended by one or more humans to be evidence, that is made into a document, and treated as a document. The latter criterion is neatly circular and Humpty-Dumptyish and depends, obviously, on the way in which the putative document is *perceived*, not on what it is.[5] The discussion of antelopes might seem very remote from the concerns of the everyday librarian, though remember that chapter 10 of the *Anglo-American Cataloguing Rules, Second Edition (AACR2)* covers artifacts and realia, the latter defined as "naturally occurring objects."

However, antelopes and other objects seem quite familiar and even homely when one contemplates digital documents, which are, when all is said and done, simply sequences of binary digits, often with no discernible boundaries. We must come up with a definition and answer the question "what is a digital document?" before we can think about all the issues arising from the use of the Web in library services. How can we select, organize, catalogue, and preserve if we have no clear idea of what constitutes the object of these activities? One obvious answer is to became Brietians—that is, to use and choose what we please and, in essence, say that an electronic document is anything we treat as a document for the purposes of selection, reference, cataloguing, and preservation. Common sense tells us two things. First, everything in a digital computer is digital, and thus it is the "documentness" of a digital document that distinguishes it from the rest of the digital world. Second, a Word document is obviously a document, whereas a program that makes it possible to read that Word document is not.

This is neither idle speculation nor definition for its own sake. Is a web page a discrete document, or does the document comprise all or any of the lower-level pages linked to it? Does the document expand to include all the separate web pages linked to the page in question and, if so, what are the boundaries of that metadocument?

The following is an entry from the admirable directory Infomine:

Japanese American Network
A collection of texts and web sites primarily about the American history that relates to Americans of Japanese ancestry and their contributions to the United States. http://www.janet.org/janet_history/ja_history.html

This seems straightforward enough. However, when you enter the site, you find the following:

HISTORY
Japanese American References
A Brief Japanese American Chronology
Bibliography of Recommended Reading

Japanese American Internment Websites
Bibliography of Books on JA Internment
Camp Harmony
Executive Order 9066
The Japanese American Internment
Japanese American Internment Memorial
Manzanar National Historical Site
Remembering Manzanar
Japanese American Exhibit and Access Project
Kooskia (Idaho) Internment Camp Project
Photos of Dorothea Lange
Children of the Camps
Conscience and the Constitution
Japanese Canadian Internment
Heart Mountain Digital Preservation Project

Japanese American War Veteran Websites
100th Battalion / 442nd Regimental Combat Team
Japanese American War Veterans Website
JA Nisei Veterans (Rae Ann Galinato)

Japanese Americans in Hawaii
Issei, Nisei, Sansei, Yonsei: JA's on Oahu

Other Japanese American History Websites
Japanese American History Archives
Nikkei Heritage Online
Concentration Camp or Summer Camp (Robert Ito)

Education Resources
Asian American Curriculum Project
A Reflection of Societal Issues and Ills
National Asian American Telecommunications Association

The Japanese American National Museum

A Brief Note to JA*Net Users:

There is often some confusion between "Japanese American" and "Japanese." In this section, we primarily give attention to the American history that relates to Americans of Japanese ancestry and their contributions to the United States.

More Links to Japanese American History

Japanese American History Forum

If you have a question about JA history, you might try posting a message in this forum, and perhaps another user may be able to help you or give you leads for an answer.

Sign the JA*Net Guestbook

Any one of these many links will take you to numerous other links—some that are part of the Japanese American Network and its various projects, and some that are completely separate. For example, a click on the "Children of the Camps" subsection of the "Japanese American Internment Websites" section will take you to a page with links to, among others, the National Asian American Telecommunications Network site (http://www.naatanet.org). That site is no more a part of the Japanese American Network (in itself a complex and elaborate structure) than is a book that is cited in another book. Note, however, that, though the mental link between book and cited book is the same as that between one website and another, the practical link is far more easily made in the case of the websites. This practicality means that the boundaries between documents are far more difficult to establish.

The question of what constitutes a digital electronic document is of greater or lesser importance depending on which aspect of library services is using the document. For example, the Infomine directory entry cited above can be seen, metaphorically, as a door to a structure with an unknown number of rooms and an unknown number of stories. The entrant to the building has only the haziest floor plan to guide her. The building's contents, what the searcher is going to find behind each interior door, range from the dimly apprehended to the completely unknown at the time of entry. Worst of all, the boundary lines between one structure and another are vague or invisible. From the point of view of the reference librarian or the directory compiler/cataloguer, a description of the door and its location may well be sufficient—to them an entrance is an opportunity. To a librarian interested in the preservation of the human record, such an indication is quite inadequate. The conservationist wants to preserve the structure and its contents, not just a description of where the front door is, or, more likely, was! So the abstruse question of defining the word "document" turns out to be vital to any plans we librarians may have to organize, make available and retrievable, and preserve the digital sequences that are designed to transmit words, symbols, images, and sounds to other human beings. Before we can organize and preserve them, we must have a clear idea of what it is we are organizing and preserving.

Perhaps the pragmatic, Brietian approach is best—digital documents are what we say they are. I would suggest a refinement of this practical approach stating that a digital document is the sum of its parts but excluding separate documents with distinctly different addresses (or other denotations) to which it is linked. In the print world, we are used to hierarchies such as

Series ➤ Subseries ➤ Monograph ➤ Chapter

in which each element may have its own author(s), title, and subject. We are also used to the ambiguities that arise when the focus of cataloguing in such a series differs from library to library. Since cataloguing codes are largely silent on this topic and, if they were not, could not override the particular needs of particular libraries, we have learned to live with the resulting confusion. Any serials librarian of any experience has hair-raising tales of the polygamous and incestuous nature of the extended families to which many serial titles belong. Therefore, we can approach the relationships between and within digital documents with some experience. In the case of the Japanese American Network site cited above, the site itself is to be found at www.janet.org. The "History" collection cited in Infomine is found at www.janet.org/ja_history.html. The subsection "A Brief Japanese American Chronology" is found at www.janet.org/ja_history/niiya_chron.html. These are relationships that we can recognize and with which we are used to dealing. The "History" collection also contains many links to other sites. One of these is the Japanese Canadian Internment site from the University of Washington library. Its address is www.library.washington.edu/subject/Canada/internment /intro.html. Not only is it a separate document, its denotation (web address) clearly shows it to be so. We can see here the beginnings of a method of demarcating web documents and one that allows the focus of the activity (cataloguing, preservation, etc.) to be at the level chosen by the individual library.

If the focus of a library's cataloguing is the "History" document in the simple example above, then the Japanese American Network site stands in the same relationship to it as a series does to a separately catalogued monograph. Further, the "Brief Chronology" is part of the catalogued electronic document in the same way as a separate paper is part of a volume of conference proceedings. The "Canadian Internment" document is best seen as what we refer to as a "related work," to be catalogued (if at all) separately with a link to the record for the "History" collection.

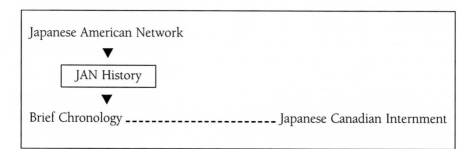

CATEGORIZING THE WEB

Even if we arrive at a satisfactory definition of "digital document" and have a clear idea of what the objects are that we wish to organize and preserve, several other questions remain. Which digital documents shall we seek to organize? Which shall we preserve? How are we to assure that the descriptions of, and access points to, digital documents actually relate to existing and accessible documents when it is well known that those documents are peculiarly subject to change and erasure?

In order to answer these questions, we need at least an outline taxonomy of the world of electronic documents (see chapter 9 for a further exploration of this topic). Most statements about electronic communication, whether laudatory or critical, tend toward generalization and the bandying-about of vast numbers, rather than being evaluative or descriptive. Whether one believes that the Web represents a quantum leap forward for humankind; that the Web is a vast wasteland; or that the Web is good in part and worthless in part, surely we can all benefit from understanding the nature of the documents and resources the Internet makes available. In that spirit, I offer the following categorization of Internet documents. What we are faced with, broadly, is:

- Ephemera
- Commercial sites
- Print-derived resources
- Electronic serials (freestanding, i.e., not derived from print)
- Digitized archives (textual, sound, and visual)
- Original creative works (textual, sound, and visual)

Ephemera

Libraries have always ruled out, consciously or unconsciously, vast areas of recorded information. We have been selective not only within formats, but have also been very selective in regard to the formats themselves that we do and do not collect. Much of the stuff that we used to ignore now shows up on the Internet and the Web. To demonstrate this, just perform a search using a search engine on any subject and review the inevitably enormous number of "hits" with a view to imagining their tangible analogues. For example, a Google search on "Andorra" done on January 8, 2002, yielded "about 1,190,000" results in 0.58 seconds. The first ten results included electronic versions of informational pamphlets on the principality in Catalan (its official language); a description of a free weekly newspaper; and an advertisement for the principality's five ski resorts. The 181st to 190th results included two real estate advertisements; a recipe for an authentic Andorran delicacy (onion salad with honey); hotel reservation information; and an advertisement for a web construction company. Later dips into the more than a million "hits" yielded a music school specializing in piano, accordion, guitar, battery drum, and trumpet; a list of Linux users in Andorra; and a statement that neither the Red Cross nor the Red Crescent have programs in Andorra.

These descriptions are not intended to belabor the point that those who put their faith in Google are doomed to disappointment or to show the futility of the free-text search engine approach. They are intended to show that the vast majority of items retrieved from the Web have analogues with the kind of ephemera (print or otherwise) that libraries have never collected. The examples given above were selected from a review of four randomly chosen sets of ten "hits" from the more than one million results yielded by the search. They are entirely typical of any such search and should worry anyone who reads of an increasing reliance on the Web for recorded knowledge and information.

There are many other kinds of digital ephemera on the Web. Personal web pages are the electronic versions of scrapbooks and diaries—of keen interest to their compilers but to few others. Then there are restaurant reviews; press releases in digital form; association and club newsletters; fairy chess tournament announcements; weather forecasts; faculty lists of Australian universities; syllabi from library schools in Italy; advertisements for chiropractic services in Costa Rica; and electronic swap meets for toy steam engines. On and on it goes—acres of the cyberworld full of ephemera. Libraries have collected this stuff indirectly (advertisements in magazines and local newspapers), sporadically (as part of clippings collections), or not at all. They have certainly never made sustained efforts to bring such materials under bibliographic control or to preserve them. Why should we start now?

There is a pervasive myth that libraries are being challenged, for the first time, by other suppliers of "information" (however defined). The truth is, as any objective look at libraries over the years will reveal, that "information" has always been available from places other than libraries and that the people who use libraries often buy their own books (and did so long before the rise of Amazon.com). The world of recorded knowledge and information has always been scattered, diverse, and characterized by mobility between various sources. Libraries have specialized in recorded knowledge and have provided information services in various ways, but there has never been a time when the library was the first place that *every* information-seeker would or should consult. Forms of communication coexist and are used to a greater or lesser extent, depending on needs, tastes, and means. If I want a weather forecast, I will use the Internet or the Weather Channel in preference to the notoriously fallible local paper, but I will use any of the three in preference to a trip to the library.

Commercial Sites (including Pornography)

I define a commercial site as one that, as its sole or primary reason for existing, attempts to sell products or services. This includes everything from Amazon.com through carinsurance.america.com to the millions of XXX-rated sites. The definition excludes sites such as that of National Public Radio (though you can buy T-shirts, coffee mugs, aprons, and other NPR tchotchkes there) and the many museum sites that offer books, postcards, and other objects for sale, since such bodies do not exist primarily to make such sales. People anxious to sell you something populate much of the electronic frontier. From e-tailers to business-to-business sites to pornographers, they are all pursuing the capitalist dream of easy profits. Ironically, there are very few who have realized that dream and many who have crashed and burned trying to sell groceries, toys, or carpeting on the Web. In fact, the concept of a new Internet-based economy now looks somewhat tattered, and even at holiday times, purchases on the Web account for a very small percentage of total sales. That percentage is rising, but it seems that it will be many years, if ever, before web commerce dominates. The only uniformly successful commercial enterprises in cyberspace are those of pornographers; the Web offers their customers certain amenities (home delivery, anonymity, secrecy) and has given pornographers access to an entirely new and huge market because of those amenities. Sellers of less gaudy business-to-consumer services cannot match the pornographers in that way.

Only a small number of specialized libraries have collected commercial information (particularly of the transient nature found on most commercial Web sites) or, in the case of those with other specializations, pornography. This enormous sector of the Web cannot be dismissed summarily and can be used with profit of one kind or another, but it does not, I would submit, fall into the collecting domain of the great majority of libraries.

Print-Derived Resources

One of the indisputably valuable sectors of the Web consists of the many documents and sites that are derived from the print industry and are dependent on the success of that industry for their very existence. These, by and large, do not present much of a technical problem either for access, bibliographic control, or preservation. In addition, print-derived sources tend to be much more stable than other websites. We know, in principle, how to catalogue and thus gain access to different format manifestations of texts and graphic publications; extending that knowledge into cyberspace is not a massive intellectual challenge. Furthermore, print-derived electronic resources have readily preserved print analogues that tend to outlast their electronic manifestations.

Electronic Journals

Most electronic journals, of course, are based on the products of a flourishing print industry. There have been many forecasts over the last decade that electronic journals will supplant print journals, but no one has as yet produced an economic model for such a major change, and there are still only a microscopic number of commercially viable true electronic journals. The problem is that the whole concept of a journal (serial assemblages of articles which are paid for in advance—whether they are ever read or not) seems inapplicable to the electronic age. Many problems in adapting to technology are caused by simply automating procedures or resources and not re-thinking the whole issue. This is the case with that widely publicized consortium, the Association of Research Libraries' SPARC (Scholarly Publishing and Academic Resources Coalition).[6] A sometimes bitter controversy—pitting scholarly journal publishers against academic librarians—has arisen over the high prices of such journals, particularly scientific, technical, and medical ones. SPARC seeks to provide a new publishing outlet for "high quality alternatives to high priced journals" in which the library consortium itself becomes the not-for-profit publisher of new, reasonably priced journals. This, of course, is opposed by the profit-based scholarly publishers.

One feels some sympathy for both sides, since libraries have suffered from high and escalating journal prices but also nourish a number of unproven myths about journal publishing and advance naive solutions to a marketplace issue. My aim here is not to debate or take sides in this long-running soap opera, but to liken the sides to two bald men fighting over a comb.[7] Why argue over who should publish, profit from, and pay for journals when the journal as such is outmoded? Print technology made it desirable to bundle articles on like topics together and set up a system in which 20 percent of the articles account for 80 percent of the reading, but libraries and other subscribers pay for the read and the unread alike. Why not, in an age of electronic communication, provide services that deliver desired articles on demand and charge the users only for the articles that are used? In such a world, the "journal" would no longer exist and publishers would be publishing (and libraries would be cataloguing and preserving) at the level of what S. R. Ranganathan called "micro-thought"—a level that we have always left to indexing and abstracting services. (See chapter 9 for a further exploration of this concept.)

Digitized Archives (Textual, Sound, and Visual)

One of the most important and valuable achievements of electronic systems is the way in which archival collections have been made available to global audiences. Those archives (which are unique by definition) have hitherto been accessible only to researchers with the means and time to travel to the physical archive itself. Parish registers are a good example of sources that can be made available to the vast web audience of family genealogists (who are second in number only to consumers of pornography).[8] A well-known example of digitized archives, the Library of Congress's American Memory Project,[9] is a vast assemblage of pamphlets and other texts, graphic items, films, sound recordings, maps, etc., that is taking advantage of digitization and the Web to give the world access to the untold riches of the LC's archival collections. The Commonwealth War Graves Commission provides a detailed listing of the millions of British Commonwealth dead of the World Wars.[10] Other institutions have created web archives of coins, stamps, posters, manuscripts, prints and drawings, early films, sound recordings, photographs, and every other conceivable means of communication, including artifacts.

There has long been a great divide between library practices (in particular, cataloguing) and archival practices. For example, in cataloguing, libraries concentrate on individual manifestations of works, while archives have been largely concerned with creating finding aids for assemblages of documents. In the twenty-odd years since the appearance of the *AACR2*, there has been some movement to bring the two cataloguing traditions closer together.[11] Although the two will always operate at different levels, there is no reason why their cataloguing practices cannot be harmonized and the results of such harmonization applied to the various parts of the American Memory Project and other such digital archives. Other methods and services in libraries and archives can come together in dealing with digitized archives and bringing their riches to general library users.

Original Creative Works (Textual, Sound, and Visual)

The advent of cyberspace has created a new environment for artists in all older media to extend and develop their art. Film, a new medium of communication a century ago, developed into an art form for directors (the French term *auteur* is particularly significant here), cinematographers, and a new breed of actors. Television, that great cultural wasteland, has not been as culturally beneficent as film, but it has given rise to some creative products by writers, actors, and documentary makers and also has provided a medium for video artists such as Nam June Paik. In the same way, there are forecasts of new breeds of creators on the Internet, including hypertext writers, digital artists, cyberpoets, and electronic musicians. When such productions belong to the same families as materials already collected and catalogued by libraries (as is the case with hypertexts), they will be collected and catalogued. Other artistic productions in cyberspace will be the province of museologists, videographers, and art collectors.

Obviously, we need a more detailed analysis of the materials available on the Internet than I have offered here and, crucially, we need more quantified analysis if we are to delineate the problem accurately and frame a response to it. Just as a beginning, we need to know which areas of cyberspace we are going to chart, catalogue, and preserve and, by inference, which areas we are going to leave to search engines and the like.

NOTES

1. The "invisible Web" may be defined as authoritative information that cannot be retrieved by standard search engines. See, for example, Chris Sherman and Gary Price, *The Invisible Web* (Medford, N.J.: CyberAge Books, 2001).

2. *The Protocols of the Elders of Zion* was a notorious, virulently anti-Semitic fraud that first surfaced in the 1920s and has proven to have great staying power. See, among others, United States Senate, Committee on the Judiciary, *"Protocols of the Elders of Zion": A Fabricated "Historic" Document: A Report Prepared by the Subcommittee to Investigate the Administration of the Internal Security Act and Other Internal Security Laws* (Washington, D.C.: Government Printing Office, 1964).

3. Michael K. Buckland, "What Is a 'Document'?" *Journal of the American Society for Information Science* 48, no. 9 (1997): 804–9.

4. Suzanne Briet, "Qu'est-ce que la documentation?" quoted in Buckland, "What Is a 'Document'?"

5. In Lewis Carroll's *Through the Looking-Glass,* Humpty Dumpty says, "When I use a word, it means just what I choose it to mean—neither more nor less."

6. Richard K. Johnson, "Effecting Change through Competition: The Evolving Scholarly Communications Marketplace," *LOGOS* 12, no. 3 (2001): 166–70.

7. Jorge Luis Borges's memorable description of the Falklands War between the United Kingdom and Argentina.

8. In January 2002, the U.K. Census Office introduced a site containing all the results of the 1901 census. The site was planned to take up to one million consultations a day. Within days, demand many times that great caused the site to collapse and be taken down for reengineering.

9. American Memory Project, at http://memory.loc.gov.

10. Available at http://www.cwgc.org.

11. See, for example, Steven Hensen, "NISTFII and EAD: The Evolution of Archival Description," *American Archivist* 60, no. 3 (1998), 284–96.

6 Reference Work in Technologically Advanced Libraries

LIBRARY COLLECTIONS

IT WAS POSSIBLE, MORE THAN A CENTURY AGO, TO DEFINE A LIBRARY'S COLLECTION AS THOSE printed texts housed in a room, building, or set of buildings. Even back then, however, many libraries possessed other carriers of knowledge and information besides books and journals. Such things as manuscripts, musical scores, and maps were commonly found in libraries, as were stereographs, prints, and other graphic items. Photographs, sound recordings, microforms, moving pictures, audiovisual materials, and realia were added as the twentieth century progressed. It is worth noting that predictions of their transformational power and the reshaping of libraries they would cause accompanied many of these new forms. It may be that the interest and enthusiasm generated by electronic technology are uniquely intense, but they are hardly unique. At the same time as library collections were expanding in size and diversity of format, interlibrary resource-sharing reached new levels because of the automation of catalogues and the rise of OCLC and other "utilities." The walls that circumscribed the libraries of 1850 have given way to a transparency and blending made possible by the intelligent and effective application of technology.

As I discussed briefly in chapter 1, the concept of a "collection" has changed utterly in a modern, technologically advanced library. It is easy to see that change as arising simply from the difference between tangible library materials (books, films, journals, maps) and electronic documents and resources. There are many contemporary Manicheans who do see the library world in exactly those simple terms, and the epic struggle between outdated print (bad) and electronic technology (good) looms large in their febrile imaginations.[1] As always, the actual facts are more complicated and nuanced. Some electronic resources, for example, do come in tangible carriers. You can purchase and store a CD-ROM just as you can purchase and store a book. Of course, you need a machine to use the CD-ROM, but then you need a machine to use a DVD, a microfiche, and a filmstrip. Moreover, many electronic resources and documents are merely the intangible analogues of tangible materials—newspapers, archives, videos, etc. A newspaper read on a screen is no less a newspaper than one read on a printed page—from the point of view of the collection developer they are the same, at least when one considers their present utility. Just as materials housed in a library are more immediately accessible than those housed in physically distinct and distant places, electronic resources owned and maintained by the library (CD-ROMs, certain e-books, etc.) are more consistently available than distant electronic resources. Far from being a simple world divided between print and electronic materials, the modern library's collections are a complex mélange of materials in many formats owned or subscribed to by the library and materials in many formats owned by others but available by a variety of means (interlibrary loan, access to remote databases). The 1990s cliché of "access not ownership" has a germ of truth (the defining characteristic of a cliché) but oversimplifies the multidimensional world of access *and* ownership that is the modern library's "collection."

The complexity of the concept of collections is further multiplied when one considers the great differences in size, mission, and concentration between different kinds of libraries. Medical, legal, and technological research libraries have different needs and demands from those of general public libraries and academic library special collections. Each of these libraries will have a technological component in its collection, but the size and nature of that component will vary greatly in different libraries.

A FALSE DICHOTOMY?

The terms "public services" and "technical services" are ingrained in our collective culture. I have never been a fan of either term or of the dichotomy they embody. This mild opposition has been rendered even milder by recent coinages such as "access services," "information delivery services," and (shudder) "interpretative services." (The latter always summons up a vision of white-faced mimes.) The two "services" have been psychologically divided for many years, and I believe this has been detrimental for service to users and for the quality of work life of librarians. "Public services" seems to imply groups of people who are uniquely suited to interaction with the users of the library; whereas "technical services" denotes a group of secretive, hidden librarians, devoted to the arcana of cataloguing and the dark world of systems. These stereotypes have led to a lack of communication and interaction and even to the belief that the two groups have different psychological profiles—one introspective and incapable of dealing with people, the other extrovert and too large-minded to be bothered with the pettifoggery of cataloguing. The truth is that each group has much to offer the other and true collaboration between them has great potential for the improvement of service to the "public"—a cause to which both should be dedicated.

THE END OF REAL REFERENCE SERVICE?

However library collections are defined, they are either inert or randomly used without the human interaction that we call reference service. Given the currently fashionable talk of "disintermediation," "live reference," and "everything being available on the Internet," it might seem that person-to-person reference service (the key element in public services as defined up to now) is on its way out; that it will go the way of the Library of Congress catalogue card and readers' advisory services. As with many other predictions concerning "virtual libraries" and the like, forecasting the "death of face-to-face reference" seems to ignore the manifest advantages and popularity of this service. It seems to me that one has to have extremely strong arguments to facilitate or allow the demise of a service that is both expected and appreciated by a wide range of library users.

In November 1876, Samuel S. Green of the Worcester Free Public Library wrote an interesting article on what we now call "reference work" in what was to become the *Library Journal*.[2] In that simpler world he wrote of "Modest men in the humbler walks of life and well-trained boys and girls" who needed "encouragement before they become ready to say freely what they want." Though there were no such things as reference librarians back then, Green summed up the question in terms that, mutatis mutandis, have much resonance today:[3]

> A hearty reception by a sympathizing friend, and the recognition of someone at hand who will listen to inquiries, even though he may consider them unimportant, make it easy for such persons to ask questions, and put them at once on a home footing.

Green's description delineates the ideal personal attributes of a reference librarian, if indirectly. These qualities are friendliness, the ability to put an inquirer at his or her ease, the realization that all questions are important to the questioner, and willingness to help. Combine these with a thorough knowledge of sources and resources and you have the recipe for the reference interview of today.

Green went on to give numerous instances of what we would now call "reference encounters" on a wide range of subjects and with all kinds and conditions of people. The common thread is the desire to help and the matching of question and source that most closely matches the expressed and unexpressed wishes of the library user. Green states, with justice, that good things flow from this "personal intercourse" between librarian and user. To paraphrase, they are:

1. After gaining the respect and confidence of the library user, the librarian can direct him to the best sources of information and foster the love of learning.
2. The librarian acquires a fuller knowledge of the collection and can use experience in developing that collection.
3. Mingling with the library's users and gaining their trust strengthens the view of the library as an indispensable institution.
4. The librarian can use the trust that good reference work engenders to elevate taste and improve reading.

No doubt this is too high-minded and Victorian for this low-minded and cynical age, but the desire to serve; to help all people; to elevate the public taste and level of learning; to consolidate the library as an essential part of the community; and, above all, to *help,* can be dismissed only at our peril. What we dealt with then, and what we deal with now, is the interaction of librarian, users, and collections.[4] There must be sympathy between librarians and library patrons; knowledge of the collections on the part of librarians; and the ability of collections to meet all the knowledge and information needs of the library's users. Inadequacies in, or lack of, any of a collection's components threaten this intricate mutual dependence. The most exalted reference skills cannot make up for seriously inadequate collections. Lack of sympathy toward the library user can make even the most knowledgeable reference librarian ineffective, even when the collections are adequate.[5] Knowing the reference collections well is important to good reference work, but so is an intimate knowledge of the wider collections. If we can use technology and electronic collections to enhance this complex structure, then so much the better for us all.

There are those who propose that technology can be employed to provide a satisfactory alternative to the nuances of the interaction between librarian and user, the librarian's familiarity with the whole range of recorded knowledge and information, and the subtleties of information- and knowledge-seeking. The fact that such proposals lack credibility has not stopped some from offering them.[6] Among the proposals aimed at replacing person-to-person reference are:

- Expert systems
- E-mail reference
- Triage service (the Brandeis model)
- Reference service by appointment
- Elimination of reference service entirely

Each of these (other than the last) has some superficial attractions and all have inherent and fatal flaws. Dave Tyckoson has analyzed and dismissed each in a magisterial article so I need do no more than state that technology can enhance but will never supplant face-to-face reference service.[7] Furthermore, if the latter were to disappear, it would be a severe and possibly fatal blow to the whole concept of library service.

REFERENCE AND VALUES

In an earlier book I advanced eight core values of librarianship.[8] I wish now to seek to relate each of those values to person-to-person reference.

Stewardship

Librarians and archivists must ensure that the human record survives and grows and must be stewards of our profession and its useful policies and practices. Though reference librarians are not always directly involved in the preservation of the records of civilization, they are, and should be, vitally concerned about the totality of that record. In particular, much useful recorded knowledge and information is lost to libraries when older reference resources are discarded in favor of newer, updated editions or other resources. It also seems that some reference librarians are concerned only with the materials housed in the reference department itself. This runs smack into one of the great circular definitions of all time: a reference book is a book housed in the reference department. The truth is that the knowledge and information sought by library users may be found in any of the collections available to the modern reference librarian—and the tangible documents in the reference department are merely the closest and most conveniently arranged. As far as electronic resources are concerned, the reference librarian has a duty to view them in the light of all other resources.

This means using them when they are the best source and eschewing them when they are not. The lazy resort to the Web first and last is the worst sort of abdication of responsibility. Charles Ammi Cutter said that the convenience of the catalogue user should always be preferred to the convenience of the cataloguer.[9] The same goes for the reference librarian and the inquirer at the reference desk. Good reference librarians are aware of and value the whole world of recorded knowledge and information—from books to maps, videos, electronic resources, and everything in between. They are concerned for all resources of all kinds and their onward transmission to posterity. They cannot, therefore, be indifferent to the fact that the inchoate nature of electronic resources and their mutability poses a preservation problem unlike anything in the last 500 years. There is a very real chance that much of what is now available electronically will not be available in a few years. By unavailable, I mean lost forever, not just "difficult to find." This is a sea change in the history of communication—or rather a reversion.

> In the mid-1500s, Bishop Diego de Landa ordered the Conquistadors to burn all the Mayan bark-cloth books they could find, because these "contained nothing but superstitions and falsehoods of the Devil." The great collection of Mayan astronomical knowledge was thus destroyed . . . Descendants of the Mayans live today in the forests of Guatemala . . . but all the knowledge their ancestors accumulated over the centuries is lost.[10]

It is not hard to see what Mayan bark-cloth books have in common with electronic resources—they were easily obliterated (from malice or inadvertence) and, once gone, were gone forever. The same could be said of all the manuscripts, papyrus rolls, etc., that predated the printed codex. If the latter proves to be a long aberration in human history, it behooves all of us to come to terms with that fact and ponder what we should do when only the electronic records of the last handful of years are available as reference sources.

In an age when a student of librarianship is as likely to take a course on Java script as a course on reference work, reference librarians should be alert to the peril that threatens their specialty. They should be even more alert when that peril is reinforced by those who believe that:

- untutored users can find everything they want and need by themselves on the Web ("disintermediation");
- reference help should be available only by appointment; and
- we do not need person-to-person reference at all.

Good stewards are custodians of cumulative professional skills and ensure that those skills are taught to their successors. This requires that reference librarians take an enlightened interest in library education and lobby for reference courses to be taught. It also requires that they take the products of LIS schools and, through example and instruction, train them to be good reference librarians with a comprehensive knowledge of sources, superior communication skills, and a commitment to reference service.

Service

Service to individuals, society, and humanity as a whole is central to all library work. Reference librarians have to be animated by a desire to help—that desire being based on sympathy for the individual and for the library's users as a group. Service is not the only motive in reference work—intellectual curiosity being a strong element for many—but it is surely the indispensable motive.

In a way, one can see person-to-person reference as the capstone in the evolution of library service. In the beginning there are collections, then those collections have to be organized, and then they have to be interpreted.

> The story is told that Aristophanes of Byzantium, who was Director [of the Library of Alexandria] from ca. 200 to 185 BC and who "working daily with the utmost drive and diligence systematically read all the books," when serving as a judge in a competition of poets held before the king, disqualified all but one on the grounds of plagiarism. Called upon by the king to prove his case, he rushed to the library and "relying just on memory," from certain bookcases produced an armful of rolls.
>
> This bravura feat may have been possible for Aristophanes of Byzantium, but after the collection had reached a certain size, ordinary readers needed the sort of help locating works that they enjoy today.[11]

That help came, of course, from the first great cataloguer—Callimachus of Cyrene—but it must also have come from Aristophanes of Byzantium and his successors in the form of what we now call "reference service." Viewed in this sense, and perceiving the continuity between libraries over more than two millennia, we can see that bibliographic control and reference work are mutually dependent and complementary. A collection, once beyond a certain size, must be organized for retrieval—a task for latter-day Callimachuses—but that organization can work only up to a point. That point is the one at which a skilled human being (a reference librarian) is needed to give guidance and assistance in using the bibliographic architecture of organization and to act as a guide, philosopher, and friend to all who use library materials.

A true service ethic treats a child's inquiry as being as important as a Nobel Prize winner's; a relevant book or electronic source as being more important than a marginally relevant electronic source or book; and makes no value judgments when it comes to either questions or answers.

Intellectual Freedom

Libraries are devoted to free inquiry and the freedom of each mind to consider any aspect of the human record. The question of intellectual freedom is essentially a clash of cultures—one inward-looking, timorous, and closed; the other outward-looking, adventurous, and open. Let this question not be muddied by reference to the question of "protecting children" (an opportunistic parrot cry of the congenitally censorious); that is, and should be seen to be, a separate discussion (and one by no means as clear-cut as it may seem). Let us consider adults and their natural and, in this country, constitutional, right to read and view whatever they wish. Instead of fearing what is unfamiliar, distasteful, or not congruent with our beliefs, we should always remember that our only allegiance as librarians is to the absolute right to free inquiry. We must let time and the tides of thought take care of that which we do not care for and, in doing so, liberate ourselves from the role of arbiters of taste or propriety and the presumption to judge, sift, and eliminate.

Surely the right to intellectual freedom is nowhere more established than in reference service. My understanding of intellectual freedom and reference is that people have the right to ask any question that does not infringe on the rights of the person being asked and that the reference librarian must be able to draw on the whole human record in order to answer that question. If that is so, person-to-person reference work calls for qualities of tact and understanding that may be difficult for many, but that are essential if free inquiry is to flourish. Areas of thought that are "sensitive" inevitably arouse strong emotions in both reference librarians and seekers of knowledge and information. How many feel completely at ease in asking for information on abortion, religion, racism, safe sex, or any other of the many topics that are the stuff of argument, dissent, and the formulation of public policy? All the more reason, then, for the reference librarian to be as neutral as humanly possible in attempting to provide factual, unbiased information and referring questioners to the best recorded knowledge.

This problem has been magnified by the advent of the Internet. In the Age of Print, publishing—and particularly scholarly publishing—provided stability and authenticity to the body of recorded knowledge and information that was the stuff of reference work. Did any reference librarian ever question the value and authenticity of the information contained in, say, an Oxford University Press reference book? In fact, it could be argued that we were, if anything, too unquestioning. No human endeavor is infallible, and the very solidity of print made us accept without question almost everything presented between blue cloth covers with gilt trim. Be that as it may, few reference librarians went far wrong in relying on the work done by the publishers, editors, and writers of the Oxford University Press, Britannica, Merriam-Webster, and thousands of others. Their one flaw lay in currency—the practicalities of the print publishing industry made the information contained in many reference books and other print sources out of date (even if slightly) on the day they were published. Too much can be made of this—there is a great deal of enduring value in the majority of reference books—but in some cases the question of currency looms large.

To get a true flavor of the predicament we are in now, compare respectable medical resources such as *Mosby's Medical, Nursing, and Allied Health Dictionary* or the *American Medical Association Encyclopedia of Medicine* with the innumerable sources of medical information and misinformation to be found on the Internet. The former have every virtue except currency; the latter may have no virtues or only the virtue of currency. Reference librarians are rightly chary of being accused of practicing medicine without a license. When it comes to printed sources of high repute, all they have to do is indicate the sources and mention their date of publication as a possible warning. When it comes to Internet resources, when does encouraging critical thinking tip over into warning people off worthless sites or sites that are not what they purport to be? We are dedicated to intellectual freedom and free inquiry, but that dedication may be sorely tested in the inchoate world of the Internet.

Rationalism

Reason and the rational approach lie at the heart of all library practice and philosophy. Idealism tempered by pragmatism is the hallmark of the mind of a true librarian. We yearn to do the right thing, but we also yearn to get things done and to deliver the best service of which we are capable. Librarians do not espouse ideas built on faith but seek that which can be proved and demonstrated to reasonable people. Reason is the basis of the ways in which we assign priorities and carry out our programs and services. It is also the intellectual bedrock of all our specialties—from collection development to cataloguing to reference services.

Although person-to-person reference service is based on the exercise of human capabilities and their attendant subjectivities, it too must be governed by reason as far as possible. This has several ramifications. Although the reference interview is a matter of human communication, it can be systematized as far as the librarian is concerned. The reference librarian should always follow certain rational ideas well entrenched in librarianship (such as proceeding from the class of question to the question itself). In this way, it is possible to ensure that what seems to the library user to be merely a helpful conversation is, in reality, a rational path to an answer. Another aspect of reference service that is subject to rational analysis is that of the sources used to provide answers. We have already looked at print (with its attributes of fixity, authenticity, and lack of currency) compared with electronic resources (with currency as their strong point). It follows that the rational approach is to use each in areas in which they are strong and to understand and explain the advantages and drawbacks of each. Moreover, an important aspect of modern reference work lies in steering library users (particularly young people) toward appropriate printed resources and teaching them to look upon electronic resources with a critical eye—i.e., exercise rationality.

One of the enduring questions of reference work is the classification of types of reference inquiry. There are commonly accepted categories—locational, library policy, data seeking, term paper advising, consultation, etc. The level of expertise required and the time to be taken obviously vary greatly depending on the type of inquiry. The rational approach is to try to ensure that each type of question is answered as efficiently and with the minimum expenditure of human resources and time necessary. The simplest situation is that of the small library in which one person is there to answer all and any questions, reference or otherwise. In larger libraries, the possibility exists of deploying different kinds of staff to deal with different kinds of reference inquiry and with the general inquiries that are made in all libraries. Few would question the fact that, if possible, purely directional ("Where is the Music Library?") and library policy ("How many books can I check out?") inquiries are best dealt with by staff or even student assistants. Few would dispute that in-depth reference consultations require librarians trained in reference work. The dispute lies in the middle ground. In a hypothetical world, one could classify and filter incoming inquiries and deflect them to finely defined classes of answerers. This may be intellectually appealing, but it is unrealistic, to say the least. If possible, it makes sense to siphon off the non-reference questions, but even those are sometimes possible lead-ins to true reference inquiries. "Where are the public terminals?" might well, on inquiry, come to be "I'm looking for good web resources on Africa." The sad truth is that such veiled inquiries most often come from the people most in need of reference service. The reason why their initial questions are vague and general can well be that they feel awkward about asking any question, fearful of being perceived as ignorant, or are simply unfamiliar with the protocols and practices of libraries. Ideally, all questions would be addressed to a human being who is sensitive to such issues and willing to seek the questions behind the question and to answer them or refer the user to someone who can.

Another aspect of the rational approach to reference service is assessment. Though there have been many studies of reference service, they tend to concentrate on factual questions and the accuracy of responses to them.[12] This is a narrow, though important, slice of reference service and really goes only to the question of the "information center" role of a library. Certainly, the accuracy of such responses should be assessed, and other common tallies (e.g., the number of questions in preset categories) should be collected systematically. But there are more difficult areas to assess, and they are among the most professional and valuable aspects of reference service. Naturally, they require sophisticated and time-consuming methods that are seen by many as being antithetical to the practical delivery of reference service. In addition, the more complex human interactions we seek to assess have inherent subjective elements that are not readily amenable to assessment. These difficulties should not deter us from conducting assessments of all our services in order to justify the funds we spend on them.

Literacy and Learning

Though librarianship is no longer book-based or inherently bound up with the love of books (something seen as central to our profession as recently as a generation ago), we are and should be concerned with the ability of people to interact with complex texts. This is not a matter of preferring print to electronic resources (or vice versa), but it recognizes the fact that human knowledge is recorded in words, images, and symbols. Although the latter two are of great importance to a minority of scholars (art historians, mathematicians, musicians, etc.), honesty compels us to recognize that learning in most disciplines is inextricably linked with the ability to decipher, understand, and learn from complex texts. (The medium in which those texts are found and preserved is a question of practical, not philosophical, importance.) Illiteracy and aliteracy are the chief enemies of learning in modern society. People who can read but do not are as shrouded in the darkness of ignorance as the truly illiterate.

Encouraging literacy is a part of reference work because reference librarians can empower individuals by steering them to classes of material beyond the exigencies of the question in hand. In other words, adding value to a reference answer can increase the impulse toward more and more reading. A good reference librarian will not only answer a question accurately, but will also suggest other readings in the area of the inquiry or in related areas. A reference query can be seen as a closed loop in which the whole story is that of a question asked and a question answered and no more. More positively, such a query can also be seen as a knock on a door, the answer being an opening of the door that leads to a lifetime of learning and the acquisition of knowledge.

Equity of Access

I have already discussed the most pervasive cliché of the day, the "digital divide." If it were not sad, it would be almost comic to see how this divide is viewed as being unique to digital information—as if such social inequities were unknown before the invention of the Internet. To those not blinded by the white light of technology, it is regrettable, but scarcely startling, that the disabled, the poor, the rural, the aged, the young, members of minorities, and other disadvantaged persons have fewer privileges than those who do not belong to any such category. Let us assume, for the sake of argument, that the digital divide is an issue to be solved, rather than a symptom of far wider social problems. There is no doubt, given that premise, that libraries can be frontline agencies in closing the divide and that reference librarians can give a great deal of assistance and training to those on the wrong side of the divide.

If you believe, as I do, that the digital divide is simply a manifestation (and by no means the most important one) of social inequities of all kinds and that the goal is equity of access to the whole range of library services, then it is clear that reference service has a vital role to play as libraries seek that goal. To take but one example, are the quality and level of reference service the same in major research libraries as they are in junior college libraries? Given the inequity of funding between these institutions, the answer is probably no. Do the students in junior colleges need more assistance and training than the students in major research institutions? The answer is probably yes. Here is the essential paradox—the service is funded adequately for people who need it the least and funded inadequately for those who need it the most.[13] Middle- to upper-class suburbs have well-stocked, well-staffed libraries, while the inner city has only the library service that dedication and battling against all the economic and social odds can supply. Good reference service should not be a matter of socio-economic class, but all too often it is. That is why it is vitally important that reference service should be provided to all to the maximum extent that it can be, and reference librarians should seek to provide that service in as equitable a fashion as is possible. Innumerable issues come to mind in this context. Are the furniture and equipment in the reference area conducive to its use by the disabled? Do students get the same level of reference service as faculty? Are the physical arrangements of the reference area people-friendly and of a type that will induce shy, comparatively uneducated people to ask questions without fear of embarrassment? The questions go on and on, but they must be asked (and asked from the user's point of view) often if the goal is equitable reference service.

It is here that the underlying altruism of most librarians comes into play and that one of the benign effects of technology is felt. That effect is the leveling of access to electronic resources. The users of the Yale University Library have access to print and other tangible collections of untold richness. The users of a junior college in a small town in central California are lucky if they have access to one five-hundredth of those resources. The difference between the number and range of electronic resources (and assistance in their use) available to these two groups is probably still great, but it is orders of magnitude less than with "traditional" resources. Another way in which technology can be used to lessen inequities in the provision of reference services is in such programs as e-mail reference, "live" (i.e., remote electronic synchronous) reference, and other ways of reaching remote users. (It should be noted that the best of these is the telephone—the most advanced and the most available network in history.) As observed previously, none of these approaches is as effective as face-to-face reference service, but they are far better than no service at all for rural, homebound, and other seekers of knowledge and information.

Privacy

Global networks and the growing involvement of technology in all aspects of life have led us to a situation in which only unexpressed thoughts are truly private. All expressions, whether in speech or writing, and all actions can be made public without our consent. There is no guarantee of privacy in e-mail communication (the most widely used application of electronic technology), but many believe that sending an e-mail is the equivalent of mailing a letter. Telephone calls are monitored and tapped; video cameras record all actions in public places in the name of security; and Inquisitor Kenneth Starr was allowed to poke into the book-purchasing habits of one of his victims, while only a few brave booksellers and civil libertarians spoke up against this egregious invasion of privacy. In such a climate, librarians' insistence on privacy might seem positively old-fashioned, but it matters in principle and in practice. We believe that people are entitled to read and view what they wish without others knowing what it is they have read or viewed. For that reason, we ensure that circulation records are not revealed to others, and that libraries are furnished with places in which people can read, view videos, and listen to sound recordings in privacy. (The aberration is the way we make computer screens visible to the casual passerby—partly for aesthetic reasons and partly because we do not trust people's use of such a "hot" medium. The small handheld computer linked to wireless networks may well be the instrument that restores privacy in the electronic arena.)

Users of reference services are entitled to privacy. This presents a practical problem. Most libraries seek to make reference areas open and welcoming, but those virtues are inimical to privacy. This can be a real problem when dealing with "sensitive" subjects or with shy, easily intimidated library users. One of the latter might well ask a question if he or she were assured that only the reference librarian would hear the question and answer. There is no formula for dealing with this issue, and we have to rely on the experience and tact of skilled reference librarians. Tactics include a low voice, body language, walking away from the desk with the library user, positioning screens so that only the user can see the results of a search, writing (rather than saying) the name of a source, and many other methods that fit the individual situation. This all centers on respect for the user and his or her right to privacy, and the kind of tact and understanding that can be developed but never taught. The ideal of the librarian as sympathetic friend, first advanced by Samuel Green 125 years ago, is still relevant in an age in which we are told "There is no privacy, get over it."

Democracy

Libraries are supremely democratic institutions. They stand for freedom, equality, and the rights of humankind. The idea that democracy depends on a well-informed electorate may be a truism, but it is true for all that. In a wider sense, democracy depends on education, and libraries are integral to education. We should always remember the words of that tough-minded thinker H. G. Wells: "Human history becomes more and more a race between education and catastrophe."[14] When Wells wrote those words, more than half a century ago, the catastrophe he foresaw was physical—the destruction of civilization through wars (especially nuclear wars) created by ignorance. Though much of the world is still threatened physically—by war, famine, flood, drought, AIDS, and overpopulation—the catastrophe we should seek to avert in the developed world is a cultural and societal one. We are far less threatened now by the thermonuclear technology of death, and far more threatened by the sedative technology of infotainment and the consequent flight from learning. Another of Wells's visions tells us of a far-distant future in which society is divided into the mass of degraded toilers called Morlocks and a minority of decadent idlers—the Eloi.[15] These are obviously projections of the state of late nineteenth-century capitalist society, but it is not too hard to extrapolate present trends to arrive at a society of Morlocks, subservient, not to toil, but to vulgar diversions that are the opposite of democracy and of the universally literate, universally empowered society to which library service should be dedicated.

Reference service is crucial to the library's struggle to improve democracy and to bring knowledge and information (free of specific charge, and free of value judgments) to all who ask. If, in this representative democracy, the people (the demos) are to show good judgment in electing their representatives, they must be educated and have access to recorded knowledge and information. They are unlikely to have the latter without the sympathetic guidance that reference librarians can supply and the critical thinking that is fostered by the higher levels of library instruction. Can anyone imagine a better illustration of democracy in action than this daily occurrence in an academic library I know well? A student from a disadvantaged background—the child of migrant farm workers who never graduated from high school—enters a state-supported library confident that someone with an advanced degree will help her in her life-changing pursuit of education, without charge, without prejudice, and without constraint.

We need to examine and affirm the core values of our profession if we are to flourish in a time of change and maintain the ethic of service to individuals and society that distinguishes our profession. In particular, we need to maintain the vital person-to-person component that has typified reference service across our history. This is an age in which human values are under strain and human contact and sympathy become more prized as they become more rare. Let us always have an open door to all and give to all the fruits of our skills, experience, and willing hearts.

NOTES

1. "Just as the method of recording human progress shifted from the quill to the printing press 500 years ago, so it is now shifting from print to digital form" (Karin Wittenborg, at http://www.lib.virginia.edu/dlbackstage/services.html).

2. Samuel S. Green, "Personal Relations between Librarians and Readers," *American Library Journal* 1, nos. 2–3 (November 30, 1876): 74–81.

3. Though there were no such things as reference librarians then, Green does refer to "the reference department" later in the paper.

4. See Michael Gorman, *Our Enduring Values* (Chicago: American Library Association, 2000), 10–12, for an expansive definition of "collections" that includes local holdings (tangible and electronic), distant holdings of books and other tangible objects, and remote electronic resources. This is the sense in which the word "collections" is used in this chapter.

5. Sympathy is "the act or capacity of entering into or sharing the feelings of another . . ." (*Webster's Third New International Dictionary*).

6. Jerry Campbell, "Shaking the Conceptual Foundations of Reference," *Reference Services Review* 20, no. 4 (winter 1992): 29–36. Steve Coffman, "Reference as Others Do It," *American Libraries* 30, no. 5 (May 1999): 54–56.

7. David A. Tyckoson, "What's Right with Reference," *American Libraries* 30, no. 5 (May 1999): 57–63.

8. Gorman, *Enduring Values.*

9. C. A. Cutter, *Rules for a Printed Dictionary Catalog,* 4th ed. (Washington, D.C.: Government Printing Office, 1904).

10. Foster Stockwell, *A History of Information Storage and Retrieval* (Jefferson, N.C.: McFarland, 2000), 11.

11. Lionel Casson, *Libraries in the Ancient World* (New Haven: Yale University Press, 2001), 38.

12. See, for example, Sharon L. Baker and F. Wilfrid Lancaster, *The Measurement and Evaluation of Library Services,* 2nd ed. (Arlington, Va.: Information Resources, 1991).

13. "Unto everyone that hath shall be given, and he shall have abundance, but from him that hath not shall be taken away . . ." (Matthew 29).

14. H. G. Wells, *An Outline of History,* rev. ed. (Garden City, N.Y.: Doubleday, 1951).

15. H. G. Wells, *The Time Machine* (1895).

7 Cataloguing in the Twenty-First Century

WHAT SHALL WE CATALOGUE?

Anglo-American cataloguing has always been concerned with methods—that is, "how to catalogue"—and has had very little reason to consider the question that now faces us: "which documents should we catalogue?" The mechanisms of publishing, materials vending, and collection development (selection) have ensured that the cataloguer has known exactly which books, journals, videos, maps, and sound recordings to catalogue and can, therefore, concern herself with policies, codes, and methods. Electronic materials are very different. We lack publishing and vending mechanisms and collection development in a digital world that is only in its infancy. Furthermore, the selector of a site to be added to the library's collections is just as likely to be the person who also performs rudimentary cataloguing for that site. This is far from a coherent professional situation, and the specialized professional skills that have served libraries and their users so well are blurred, weakened, and ineffective. This is not a criticism of librarians, but of library administrators and leaders—they have failed to bring clear analysis and logic to bear, relying instead on clichés, slogans, and skewed priorities. Each of the latter is a product of the kind of exceptionalism that arises from the apocalyptic view of the "information revolution." In cataloguing, above all, the fact that we are at the latest stage of a very long evolutionary process should be crystal clear.

ACHIEVING UNIVERSAL BIBLIOGRAPHIC CONTROL

The great irony of our present situation is that we have reached near-perfection in the bibliographic control of "traditional" library materials at the same time that the advent of electronic resources is seen by some as threatening the very existence of library services—including bibliographic control. Before considering the question of "cataloguing the Web and the Internet," it is salutary to review the great achievements of the past thirty years and put our present situation in their context. The international library community was only beginning to dimly discern the possibilities of the interconnection of international standardization and library automation when the ideal of "universal bibliographic control" (UBC) was first advanced thirty years ago.[1] International standardization was at a very early stage (far closer to a vision than a reality), and UBC's ideal of each item being catalogued once in its country of origin—the resulting record being made available to the world community—seemed far from practical realization. Records were exchanged between countries (mostly between national libraries), but in a most inefficient manner—print on paper— and since they resulted from different cataloguing codes and practices, were integrated into catalogues with great difficulty. The choice was between incorporating international records without alteration—something that degraded the catalogue very quickly—or doing such extensive revision (and retyping) that it would have been cheaper and quicker to catalogue the item oneself from the start. MARC (machine-readable cataloguing) was still in its infancy when UBC was proclaimed as an ideal.[2] The International Standard Bibliographic Description (ISBD) was still being drafted.[3] Cataloguing rules in different countries lacked a common basis for the assignment and form of access points ("headings") and adhered to different descriptive practices, despite the Paris Principles.[4] How have we progressed so far in a few decades? What has brought us nearer to universal bibliographic control than anyone would have dreamed possible thirty years ago? Analysis of the facts shows that it was the confluence of a need (the need of national and research libraries throughout the world for less expensive and more current cataloguing) and a means (automation, and more specifically, MARC).

We have traveled a very long road. The idea of a universal bibliography is nearly as old as the field of bibliography itself.[5] The idea of achieving economies in bibliographic control by sharing catalogue records between libraries (cooperative cataloguing) or purchasing catalogue records for other (usually national) libraries goes back to at least the mid-nineteenth century. In fact, the American librarian Charles Coffin Jewett drew up his cataloguing rules (in the 1850s) specifically for a proposed scheme by which the Smithsonian Institution would produce "separate, stereotyped titles" to be used in the catalogues of American libraries.[6] In this scheme and in the hugely successful Library of Congress catalogue card service and the *National Union Catalog* to which Jewett's concept gave rise, we can see bibliographic needs and desires that lacked only an appropriate technology if they were to be met.

In hindsight, it is easy to believe in a trajectory of inevitability that makes MARC, the ISBDs, *AACR2,* and other vehicles of international bibliographic standardization seem more the result of historical forces than of the often faltering and separate steps that actually occurred. Each of these three standards had original purposes that were quite different from their eventual impact on international standardization. MARC was originally brought into being to facilitate the creation of Library of Congress catalogue cards on demand. The ISBD evolved from the Standard Bibliographic Description (SBD) drawn up by a committee appointed as one of the two chief results of the International Federation of Library Associations' International Meeting of Cataloguing Experts (IMCE) in 1969.[7] The SBD was seen, among other things, as a means of standardizing the *presentation* of descriptive data so that it could be machine-translated into MARC (hence the stylized and individual punctuation). *AACR2* was the culmination of decades of effort to bring uniformity to cataloguing practices in the English-speaking world, and, particularly, to reconcile British and North American descriptive cataloguing practices. Each of these three standards metamorphosed and had an impact far beyond the anticipation of all but the most far-sighted. It is instructive to recall how and why each developed and expanded, because we need to understand that the bibliographic world (just like the real world) is full of unintended consequences and the ripples from a stone thrown in one part of the bibliographic pond may eventually cover it all.

The MARC format is, by any standard, a historic achievement. It has been the main force in international standardization from a practical point of view. It is literally the engine that has made UBC possible. The journey from the caterpillar of the automation of card production to the beautiful butterfly of today has been long and largely successful. It is worth pointing out, however, that MARC's origins and original purposes (including being a carrier format rather than the way in which bibliographic information is stored and manipulated) have created drawbacks that should hardly be surprising when one considers we are dealing with a nearly 35-year-old standard. The structure of MARC is that of the catalogue card, when computer systems call for a different approach. Nevertheless, the facts are that:

- There are tens of millions of MARC records in the world
- MARC is accepted and used throughout the world
- MARC is the basis for almost all automated bibliographic systems (including commercially produced systems)

- No practically feasible or demonstrably better system has been advocated. (XML and other "mark-up" systems merely substitute symbols for MARC tags and codes—losing detail in the process, scarcely an intellectual breakthrough.)

It should be unnecessary to point out that MARC is merely a *framework* standard—that is, it is a way of storing and making manipulable data that has been formulated in accordance with *content* standards (cataloguing codes and the like). I would not bother to point this out were it not for the frequent references to "MARC cataloguing" in writings about metadata and "simplified" cataloguing.[8] There is, of course, no such thing as "MARC cataloguing"—MARC is simply the way in which we encode the results of the cataloguing process and has little or no influence on that process.

ISBD

One of the two documents studied at the IMCE was a comparison of descriptions from cataloguing agencies throughout the world.[9] The document revealed great similarities in the information found in such descriptions and the order in which that information was presented. It found differences in the abbreviations used and other stylistic matters (mainly due to language differences) but was able to propose a conflation of the descriptions that formed the basis of what became the SBD and later the ISBD. The idea was originally to create a basis for agreement across cataloguing codes on the relatively non-contentious matter of descriptive data. Soon, however, this was supplemented by the idea that universally used distinctive punctuation, clearly identifying the areas and elements of the SBD, would not only aid in the understanding of bibliographic data in unfamiliar languages but could also be used in automatic translation of that data into MARC records. It is no coincidence that the areas and elements of the ISBD correspond exactly to the relevant fields and subfields of the MARC format.

In accordance with the theme of stumbling toward standardization, it should be noted that both MARC and the ISBD were developed initially for books and only later generalized into standards for all types of library material.

AACR2

The second edition of the *Anglo-American Cataloguing Rules* (AACR2) is, in fact, nothing of the sort. It was politically expedient at the time to identify this new code as a revision of the previous *Anglo-American Cataloging Rules* (1968), but

AACR2 is completely different from its predecessors in important ways.[10] One need only cite the facts that *AACR2* is a single text (unlike its predecessors, which came in North American and British versions); is the most complete working out of the ISBD for materials of all kinds; and represents the triumph of Lubetzkyan principles, which the first *AACR* signally did not. Be that as it may, *AACR2* quickly transcended even the historic achievement of being a unitary English-language cataloguing code to become the nearest approach to a world code we have. In the words of the introduction to the Italian translation of *AACR2*:[11]

> Le *Regole di catalogazione*, nella loro seconda edizione, sono il codice più diffuso nel mondo (sono state pubblicate in gran numero di lingue diverse) e l'unico che—di fatto—svolga le funzioni di codice catalografico internazionale. [The *Cataloguing Rules,* in their second edition, are the world's most widely used (they have been translated into numerous different languages) and the only rules that are, de facto, an international cataloguing code.]

This state of affairs is partly due, of course, to the dominance of the English language (in its various manifestations) in the modern world. It is also due, in part, to the fact that *AACR2* represents the most detailed working out of the principles of author/title cataloguing set forth in the Paris Principles and based on the analysis and pioneering work of Seymour Lubetzky.[12] *AACR2* is also the first application of the ISBD family of standards to all library materials.

Here we stand then, on the brink of universal bibliographic control for all "traditional" (i.e., nonelectronic) materials with a universally accepted format for exchanging bibliographic data, a universally accepted standard for recording descriptive data, and a quasi-universal cataloguing code that is either in use in, or influencing the codes of, most of the countries in the world. Is there any reason *in principle* why we should not bring electronic documents and resources into this architecture of bibliographic control? The answer is no. Are there *practical* reasons why this task is formidable? The answer is yes.

CATALOGUING ELECTRONIC RESOURCES

I have written and spoken elsewhere about the problems posed by electronic resources and the proposed "metadata" approach to bringing them under a form of bibliographic control.[13] I will try here to summarize the arguments put forward in those papers and to propose a direction that I advocate for a new age of bibliographic control.

The first issue is that of the electronic resources themselves. Some are closely analogous to print documents—this is hardly surprising, since many electronic documents are derived from print documents. Moreover, there is an established pattern of new technologies adopting the outward signs and structures of previous technologies—just think of radio news "headlines" and of television "magazines" with their "front pages." We even refer to elements of websites as "pages." Other electronic documents (particularly websites) are quite dissimilar and therefore do not immediately seem to be amenable to existing bibliographic control structures. On reflection, however, we can see that there is a commonality between documents that embraces all formats. Electronic documents have titles, dates, texts and illustrations, "editions," "publishers," relationships to other documents (electronic and otherwise), "authors," contributors, and corporate bodies associated with them.[14] We know well how to deal with each of these bibliographic elements, how to record them, how to exercise vocabulary control, and how to create MARC records that can be integrated into library catalogues. Why then have many people either despaired of bringing electronic documents under bibliographic control or advocated solutions such as metadata, expert systems, and sophisticated search engines as alternatives to cataloguing? I believe there are a number of answers to this question (not excluding ignorance), but the most important ones center on the perceived characteristics of documents on the Internet.

The attributes of a well-regulated library are well known to us all. They are organization, retrievability, authenticity, and fixity. There are those who claim that electronic documents and sites (assemblages of electronic documents) are different in kind and not just degree from all the other formats that human beings have used to communicate and preserve knowledge across the centuries. (This is not a new phenomenon—just think of the semi-hysteria in North American libraries over audiovisual materials in the 1960s and 1970s. Then as now, audiovisual materials were thought to call for special and different cataloguing rules, specially trained librarians, and the transformation of the library into a "resource center." The tumult died out as people came to their senses and integrated audiovisual materials into their collections and cataloguing rules. We still have the Library of Congress rather than the Resource Center of Congress.) The strongest support for this notion of exceptionalism comes from the evanescence and mutability of electronic documents. These characteristics, which any true librarian deplores, are really the logical outcome of the history of human communications—each format produces more documents than its predecessor, and each is less durable than its predecessor.[15] It takes a long time to make many copies of stones bearing carved messages, but those messages can be read millennia later. You can send an e-mail message from Fresno to Addis Ababa in the twinkling of an eye, but that message may be expunged in a second twinkling. Many electronic documents are like those subatomic particles that are only known because scientists can see where they have been during their micro-milliseconds of existence. Let me pose a deep philosophical question—does an e-mail message exist if it is deleted unopened?

AN ALTERNATIVE LIBRARY UNIVERSE

There is another important difference between electronic documents and all the types of library material that preceded them. It centers on how electronic resources come to our notice. Here is a short fable.

> There is an alternative universe in which there are books but no electronic documents. In that universe librarians have no control over the books that they purchase—no selection policies, no approval plans, and no collection development criteria. All these have been replaced by several trucks pulling up every hour, day and night, to the library's loading dock and depositing heaps of unordered and unwanted books—mostly from unheard-of publishers, vanity presses, and basement self-publishers. Some of those books might be of interest and use, but which ones are they; how do librarians and library users find them; and what on earth do they do with all the rest? In this alternative universe, librarianship becomes a much more random, disorganized process than anything we know. The library would send out squads of trained personnel to root through the piles looking for worthwhile items to be catalogued and shelved. But wait! This is an alternative universe, and having selected 100 books from the piles and fully catalogued and organized them, librarians come back the next day to find that 25 of them have vanished and 25 have changed their titles! Meanwhile, the piles of books outside the library keep growing and shape-shifting, and for every 100 books the library SWAT team rescues, 200 are added by the unending delivery trucks. Small wonder that, in the alternative universe, librarians are careworn and cataloguers neurotic.

If you take that alternative universe and substitute electronic documents for books, you have a taste of what we are trying to deal with in bringing electronic documents under bibliographic control. There are too many of them; some of them vanish after being recorded; some change their attributes; some are inauthentic or are not what they purport to be; some cannot be found; and there is no filtering out of the ephemeral and the meretricious (as is done by the publishing and selling industries for books and other nondigital materials). I believe that the idea of "cataloguing the Web" is not only unattainable but also undesirable—most of what is on the Web does not merit the expense and the time of cataloguing. The questions are, of course, which electronic documents are worth cataloguing and how many of them are there? I have noticed in chapter 5 that most statements about electronic communications tend toward generalization and the bandying about of vast numbers rather than being evaluative or descriptive. Whatever one's opinion of web pages and other electronic resources, surely we can all benefit from understanding the nature of the documents and resources the Internet makes available.

I have already given an outline description of the Internet's resources in chapter 5. We need a more detailed and enumerated analysis of the Web than I have offered there. We need to know which areas of cyberspace we are going to chart and catalogue and, by inference, which areas we are going to leave to search engines and the like. These will not be easy studies, but facts are a far better basis for planning than are the techno-boosterism and hand-waving that characterize most discussions of these topics.

If we can reach the point where we have decided which electronic documents and resources we are to bring under bibliographic control, two important questions still remain. Which standards shall we use? How is the cataloguing to be organized?

METADATA

The first question brings me to the topic of metadata. The term means "data about data"—a meaningless concept as stated that, taken literally, would embrace library cataloguing, even though metadata has been explicitly conceived as something that lacks most of the important attributes of cataloguing. The idea behind metadata is that there is some "third way" of organizing and giving access to electronic resources that is approximately halfway between cataloguing (expensive and effective) and keyword searching (cheap and ineffective). Furthermore, it is alleged that authors, webmasters, publishers, and others lacking any knowledge of cataloguing can supply such low-level bibliographic data.

It is entirely possible, since the original concept of metadata did not originate among librarians, that no consideration was given to the use of "traditional" cataloguing, and, even though librarians are now involved in the projects, the idea that electronic resources cannot be catalogued using existing standards may already be firmly entrenched. Nevertheless, the fact is that electronic bibliographic entities have attributes that are similar to those of other bibliographic entities. It is perfectly possible to catalogue electronic resources in such a way that the resulting records can be fully integrated into library catalogues. There is an ISBD for electronic resources that has formed the basis of the revision of chapter 9 of the *AACR2* (though regrettably the Joint Steering Committee for the *AACR2* has not followed the prescriptions of the ISBD(ER) in all cases, as it is supposed to do).[16] Electronic resources have titles and creators (authors) that can be used to provide standard access points; they have subjects that can be expressed in classification numbers and subject headings; and all that data can be incorporated into a MARC record. In short, if one of the justifications for the invention of metadata is that it is needed to facilitate access to electronic resources in the absence of cataloguing standards, that justification is flat wrong.

Perhaps the decision has been made almost without thinking it through. This decision appears to be that since "traditional cataloguing" is too expensive, there must be a compromise—the third way—that will give the benefits of cataloguing without the effort or expense. In the words of the introduction to the final report of the Nordic Metadata Project:[17]

> Many specialists believe that any metadata is better than no metadata at all—
> we do not need to stick with the *stringent quality requirements and complex formats*
> *of library catalogue systems*. Instead, it is possible to live with something simple,
> which will be easily understandable to publishers, authors and other people
> involved with the publishing of electronic documents [emphasis added].

This is one of the few mentions in this long report of the perceived need for, and the nature of, metadata as an alternative to cataloguing. It is taken for granted that there is something between "stringent quality requirements" and no quality at all, and that there is something between "complex formats" and almost no format at all.

THE DUBLIN CORE

It seems to be generally accepted that the Dublin Core is the most developed application of metadata and is on the verge of being generally accepted. It was developed by OCLC at its headquarters in Dublin, Ohio, and named for that municipality. It consists of fifteen labeled descriptive elements. Cursory analysis shows us that each of these elements has its counterparts in the MARC format and that the content of each of them is governed by codes in either MARC fixed-length fields, cataloguing codes/ISBDs, or subject heading lists/thesauri. Of course, the Dublin Core and other metadata "standards" provide a framework for holding bibliographic data but no guidance on how to formulate those data. In short, it is a subset of MARC and nothing more. No bibliographic database of any significant size could possibly work if filled with Dublin Core records containing random data without vocabulary control and standard presentation. The only reason why metadata schemes have not yet met with their inevitable collapse and consequent dismissal is that none of them has been applied to databases of sufficient size as to demonstrate their hollowness. Writings on metadata are full of references to the complexity of the MARC format and of cataloguing codes, which is always presented as being a bad thing. It is worth pointing out that that format and those codes are complex because the bibliographic world is complex. Contrary to rumor, cataloguers do not invent rules to deal with situations that will never occur. The idea that this complex world embodied in millions of bibliographic entities can be reduced to data entered by the untrained into fifteen categories is simply preposterous.

The Dublin Core is said to have the following positive attributes.[18]

- It is very simple to learn;
- has repeatable elements;
- has optional elements;
- can be extended for more complex applications;
- can be embedded invisibly in web pages; and
- is recognized by the World Wide Web Consortium.

These are all true, but are scarcely relevant to the basic concerns about metadata, since none speak to the central points of the content of the bibliographic record or of the limited nature of the subset that the fifteen elements represent.

The literature on metadata reveals a divergence between proponents of the original simplicity of the concept and proponents who think that metadata need to be normalized and subjected to vocabulary control. This discussion boils down to a choice between, on the one hand, an inexpensive and ineffective form of cataloguing in which the fifteen elements of the Dublin Core are filled with unqualified and uncontrolled free text, and, on the other hand, an expensive and more effective form of cataloguing in which at least some of the elements of the Dublin Core are filled with normalized controlled data decided on the basis of professional examination of the resource. Such human intervention would not in all probability be as time-consuming and expensive as full cataloguing, but it would certainly go beyond the simplicity and inexpensiveness desired by those who take the minimalist point of view.

A CATALOGUING PYRAMID?

My inclination has been to dismiss the Dublin Core (as an attempt to reinvent the wheel as something other than round) and to advocate the full application of library or archival cataloguing to those electronic resources that we deem worthy of such treatment. It may be, however, that we could have several layers of treatment depending on the value we assign to the various electronic resources. Such a system would be a pyramid, with the apex occupied by that relatively small proportion of electronic resources that will merit full cataloguing according to existing standards. The next level could be that of enriched Dublin Core records with data in applicable fields being subject to vocabulary control. Then there would be those electronic resources with uncontrolled Dublin Core elements. The last layer would be the huge number of electronic resources that would be retrievable, if at all, by search engines using free-text searching.

COOPERATIVE CATALOGUING OF ELECTRONIC RESOURCES

My second question was "how is the cataloguing of electronic resources to be organized?" It centers on how to proceed in identifying "worthwhile" materials, in creating and maintaining the databases that will result, and in coordinating the national effort. Again, we have choices. The first is a grand plan such as the Library of Congress's action plan called "Bibliographic Control of Web Resources."[19] The second is a grassroots movement in which individual libraries and librarians and groups of libraries choose and catalogue the documents, resources, and sites that it has been agreed are worthwhile. Both approaches call for a common understanding of which types of resources are to be catalogued and agreements on the standards to be used. Perhaps the answer lies in national and international agreements that foster and coordinate individual action but do not inhibit it. This approach will be in many ways a reprise of the history of libraries. Individuals and individual libraries built collections, one choice at a time, over many years. It was not until much later that union catalogues and library collectives brought those individual collections into national, and later international, systems. The difference this time is that the benefits of the work of individual libraries and groups can be made available to all contemporaneously. Let a thousand cataloguing projects bloom, and record by record, collection by collection, worthwhile Internet resources will be organized and made available in what will ultimately come to be international systems and databases based on internationally agreed standards.

PRESERVATION

When it comes to the question of bringing the Internet into bibliographic control, the elephant in the room is that of preservation of the human record. Supposing we solve all the problems of bibliographic standardization and the organization of a massive international effort, what is the point if the resources identified and catalogued are not preserved? Those with more faith than I look to gigantic electronic archives maintained by governments and private companies that will ensure the indefinite survival of the electronic records of humankind. This idea seems implausible when one looks at the cost of such archives, the dizzying rate of technological change, the need for the archives to be eternal, and the lack of interest outside the library and archive professions in the onward transmission of the human record. We can, of course, ignore the problem and hope that it all turns out right in the end—after all, that is what we are doing now. Alternatively, we could turn to the only known way of preserving massive numbers of texts and images—print on acid-free paper. If you are inclined to dismiss that suggestion out of hand, I would recommend that you explore the financial and cultural costs of the alternatives and keep an open mind.

In summary, when we get beyond all the pomposity and technobabble that dominate discourse on electronic documents and their bibliographic control, we can see real problems and real issues. What are we going to do about identifying and making accessible the valuable records of humanity that are only available in electronic form? How are we going to deal with the mutability and evanescence of those records? How are we going to preserve those resources and transmit them to posterity? We will only answer these questions if we employ wisdom and insight, understand the lessons of history, and work with the interests of all our users, present and future, in mind.

NOTES

1. Franz Georg Kaltwasser, "Universal Bibliographic Control," *Unesco Library Bulletin* 25 (September 1971): 252–59.

2. Henriette Avram, "The Evolving MARC System: The Concept of a Data Utility," in *Clinic on Library Applications of Data Processing,* 1970 (Urbana: University of Illinois Press, 1971), 1–26.

3. Michael Gorman, "Standard Bibliographic Description," *Catalogue & Index* 22 (summer 1971): 3–5.

4. A. H. Chaplin, "Cataloguing Principles: Five Years after the Paris Conference," *Unesco Library Bulletin* 21 (May 1967): 140–45.

5. Konrad Gesner [1516–1565], *Biblioteca universalis, sive, catalogus omnium scriptorum locupletissimus, in tribus linguis, Latina, Graeca, & Hebraica* . . . (Zurich: Apud Christoph Froschauer, 1545).

6. Charles Coffin Jewett [1816–1868], *On the Construction of Catalogues of Libraries, and Their Publication by Means of Separate, Stereotyped Titles,* 2nd ed. (Washington, D.C.: Smithsonian Institution, 1853).

7. "Report of the International Meeting of Cataloguing Experts, Copenhagen," *Libri* 20, nos. 1–2 (1970): 105–37.

8. See, for example, http://www.nyu.edu/library/bobst/research/tsd/nonmarc.htm, which refers to the (New York University) Bobst Library's "non-MARC cataloging (aka metadata)."

9. Michael Gorman, "Bibliographical Data in National Bibliography Entries: A Report on Descriptive Cataloguing Made for UNESCO and IFLA," final revised version [1968]. Working paper 2 for the International Conference of Cataloguing Experts, Copenhagen, 1968.

10. *Anglo-American Cataloging Rules,* North American text (Chicago: American Library Association, 1968); *Anglo-American Cataloguing Rules,* British text (London: Library Association, 1968).

11. *Regole di catalogazione Angloamericane,* 2. ed., revisione del 1988 (Editrice Bibliografica, 1997), vii.

12. *The Future of Cataloging: Insights from the Lubetzky Symposium* (Chicago: American Library Association, 2000).

13. Michael Gorman, "Metadata or Cataloguing?: A False Choice," *Journal of Internet Cataloging* 2 (1999): 5–21; Michael Gorman, "Metadata—Hype and Glory" [unpublished], proceedings of the ALCTS Pre-Conference on Metadata, Chicago, June 2000.

14. "Author" is defined as "the person chiefly responsible for the intellectual or artistic content of a work" (*AACR2,* "Glossary").

15. Hans Wellisch, "Aere perennius," in *Crossroads: Proceedings of the First National Conference of the Library and Information Technology Association* (Chicago: American Library Association, 1984), 22–34.

16. For ISBD(ER), see *International Standard Bibliographic Description for Electronic Resources* (Munich: K.G. Saur, 1997).

17. See http://linnea.helsinki.fi/meta/nmfinal.htm (dated July 1998).

18. See http://www.adam.ac.uk/adam/metadata.html (dated December 1997).

19. See http://lcweb.loc.gov/catdir/bibcontrol/draftplan.html.

8   Challenges of the Future

SOME OF THE EARLIER CHAPTERS IN THIS BOOK HAVE DISCUSSED THE FINANCIAL, BIBLIO-graphic, social, and physical problems that afflict libraries today and the challenges with which we must deal. Together they add up to an intimidating, if not exceptional, agenda that, if not separated into its parts and thought about coherently, could well overwhelm us. There is little evidence that the latter will happen, however. In particular, it is far more likely that electronic documents and resources will find their level and rightful place in future library services and programs.

One danger, almost entirely of our own making, looms far larger than the agenda previously discussed. *If* librarians and others persist in seeing the advent of electronic documents and resources as the Second Coming of Gutenberg and *if* we continue to behave as if we are in an exceptional and transformational time without basing that belief and those actions on a clear-headed examination of reality, we could provoke an unnecessary cataclysm. In that event, there is no overestimating the consequences of a feckless disregard of the challenges posed by electronic communication and digitization—a fecklessness that, alas, is all too common in our and related fields. It takes the form of blithe assumptions about the potential and economics of digitization and leads to policies and actions that ignore practical, financial, and technological realities.

> Now there are new utopian visions of the universal virtual library, where the user can surf through cyberspace and find all of human knowledge waiting to be accessed.[1]

These utopian visions have such a tenacious hold on the minds of many librarians and commentators that they press on, blinded by the glamour of the new to the enormous financial investments (on digitization, equipment, networks, cataloguing, etc.) that would be required to get us anywhere near the "universal virtual library." There are many reasons why we are as far away from that universal digital library as we are from intragalactic space flight, and many of the obstacles to its achievement cannot be overcome without unknowable and incredible innovations in technology and the expenditure of unthinkable sums of money. To pursue the space metaphor, it is as if we talk and write incessantly about trips to Alpha Centauri and act as if such trips were imminent. All the while we are doing the library equivalent of scratching around in the nearer parts of the solar system that is the reality of human space exploration. It is good to reach for the stars, but not when it is at the expense of thinking about real terrestrial problems and issues.

The telecommunications company Qwest ran advertisements a few years ago that showed a ravaged man checking into a sleazy motel in the back of beyond and being informed that "every movie ever made" was available in his in-room entertainment. (Another commercial showed him in an even more gruesome setting being promised every sound recording ever made.) His question, quite reasonable under the circumstances, was "How is this possible?" Good question and, of course, the answer is "it isn't." Between a third and a quarter of all movies ever made have vanished and only a fraction of the survivors are available online. There are almost insuperable problems having to do with economics, copyright, technology, and demand that militate against achieving what Qwest dramatized in its commercial. The advertisements close with the fatuous injunction to "ride the light," whatever that might mean. All this is reminiscent of the notorious IBM advertisement in the 1990s concerning a vineyard owner in Tuscany who claimed to have revolutionized his business by consulting the library of Indiana University, which IBM had "put online." It had (and has) done nothing of the sort, nor has any other company done as much for any other research library. The idea of selling the sizzle and not the steak is a tried-and-true basis for advertising, but it is usually based on the existence of a steak, no matter how small and unappetizing. In these cases, there is no steak at all and, apparently, corporate corruption now extends to flagrant public lies that are never challenged. Why is it acceptable to make such inflated claims about digital communication—claims that would be the subject of outrage and litigation in any other area of human endeavor? These commercials are only a small if very public example of our society's inability to analyze and communicate the actual facts of any public policy issue. After all, we live in a world in which national health care hinges on the vapid conversation of two fictional characters and not at all on the facts of the matter or the needs of the citizenry. It is the nature of advertising to exaggerate, but in the case of modern communications technology, the distance between the hugely inflated claims and reality is wide, widening, and unbridgeable.

Jeff Rutenbeck, associate professor in the Department of Mass Communications and Journalism Studies at the University of Denver, has advanced the notion of "five challenges" that we have to face in the "information age" if computer technology and digitization are to be beneficial influences on society.[2] They center on the basic characteristics of digital documents and electronic communication and the ways in which those characteristics influence the use of the technology. His five challenges are:

- Malleability
- Selectivity
- Exclusivity
- Vulnerability
- Superficiality

I will use each of these as a departure point for a discussion of the use of electronic documents and resources in today's libraries and suggest ways in which libraries can respond to the problems and dilemmas with which we are confronted. Though Professor Rutenbeck approaches the topic from the standpoint of an expert in communications, his thoughts on the nature of electronic documents and our use of them are directly pertinent to libraries and the future of libraries. Moreover, the challenges he outlines speak to the issues that must be resolved if libraries are to progress and thrive.

When it comes to the various issues raised by the changing nature of human communications today, it is comparatively simple to describe the environment in which libraries operate and the issues concerning digitization and electronic communication with which we have to deal.

> In addition to hundreds of millions of books and other library resources, there are millions of digital documents and resources in existence (if only for a short or unpredictable time in some cases) and millions more being created.

> Some of those documents and resources are derived from nonelectronic publishing; some have analogues in "traditional library materials"; others have analogues in nonelectronic materials with which libraries have never been concerned; and others are uniquely electronic, having no origins, parallels, or possibility of existing in a nonelectronic form.

It is thought that some electronic documents and resources will supplant nonelectronic library materials and other forms of communication, but no one knows exactly which these are, and experiments such as e-books increasingly seem like blind alleys.[3]

No satisfactory plans have yet been developed to make worthwhile electronic documents and resources readily available in a consistent and comprehensive manner. The many and fatal shortcomings of search engines are, apparently, irremediable. This has been demonstrated in real life by our experience with "advanced" and "second-generation" search engines such as Google.

No satisfactory plans have yet been developed to preserve the worthwhile records of humankind that are available only in electronic form.

No satisfactory consensus definition of "worthwhile" as used in the preceding two sentences has yet been developed.

Computer technology is developing and changing at a dizzying speed.

There is very little evidence of any slackening of demand for "traditional" library services, collections, and buildings, or that electronic services can replace "traditional" services to any important extent.

The economic impact of all of the foregoing on libraries has been vast (if largely uncharted) and no satisfactory response to that impact has yet been developed.

Despite the cloud of unknowing that permeates these statements, most writers on, and administrators of, libraries either concentrate on only one or a few of these issues or, more often, simply ignore them. For example, merely noting (as most of us do in our annual reports) that libraries have to do more with less by devoting an ever-larger portion of their budgets to electronic resources while continuing to support the demand for nonelectronic services does nothing to resolve the ever-greater dilemma. Nor does the other common response, which is to shrink and starve nonelectronic services to increase the electronic. This is a time for hard questions to be asked and concrete solutions advanced, for knowledge to replace supposition, and for the true interests of library users (now and in the future) to be put before fads and technological fantasies. If electronic documents and resources had the attributes of tangible library materials (authenticity, fixity, preservability, and standardized denotations), we would not be faced with the challenges advanced by Professor Rutenbeck. The plain truth is that almost all of our challenges and issues have their roots in the nature of electronic documents and their virtues (speed, contemporaneity, etc.) and vices (mutability, fragility, etc.).

MALLEABILITY

By this, Rutenbeck means that we can and do change electronic documents without regard to their intellectual integrity or the necessity to preserve the original content. We often fail to appreciate the role that the authenticity of documents plays in our society and in the whole architecture of knowledge and learning. The subject of authenticity pervades our lives, from the importance of signatures on a printed legal document to the patient scholarly unraveling of the exact text and exact meaning of religious documents like the Bible and quasi-religious documents like the U.S. Constitution. If a legal document such as a will or mortgage becomes the subject of a contested trial, the question of its authenticity precedes, and is the inescapable prelude to, any question as to its meaning. If the text of such a document were not demonstrably what it claimed to be and the signatures on it not demonstrably those of the persons concerned, no fair legal proceeding could take place. Arguments rage over interpretations of the Constitution but not about the accuracy or authenticity of the 4,400 words that make up that document. Whether you are a "strict constructionist" or someone who believes in the evolution of constitutional meaning, you will be arguing from an agreed text with no doubts about its authenticity or provenance.

Reconciling the complicated manuscripts and proofs of the text of James Joyce's novel *Ulysses* has been a cottage industry for several decades—one that shows no sign of reaching a universally accepted conclusion.[4] Reconciling the various texts, manifestations, and translations of the Bible has been a major industry for centuries. Though the Bible differs in many ways from *Ulysses*—after all, we have one undisputed author and a body of authenticated, if massively confusing, manuscripts and page proofs for *Ulysses*—the idea of reconciliation is the same in both cases. It involves establishing an authentic text, on the basis of which scholarship and exegesis can proceed. The Joyce industry is larger than most such literary enterprises, and the Bible industry is the grandmother of them all. Neither is at its best when focusing on variant texts. *Ulysses* is the masterpiece of a person widely considered to be one of the greatest writers of the twentieth century. The Bible is considered to be the word of God by millions and, at least, divinely inspired by millions more. How can we arrive at pronouncements on either book without having an authentic text? The answer is, of course, that the known flaws in each text are accepted and discounted by the vast majority and are not seen as fatal to an understanding of the meaning of each. In other words, we can live with a degree of inauthenticity as long as there is a sufficiently high level of authenticity. Let us suppose that the "authenticity level" of *Ulysses* is 98 percent, and that of the Bible is 95 percent. Such percentages are clearly acceptable to the vast mass of readers (other than those, one assumes, who believe in the "inerrancy" of the Bible and must therefore require a belief in a completely authentic text). However, suppose that "authenticity" level were only 50 percent or 25 percent. How could one book be proclaimed a masterpiece and the other the word of God?

The authenticity of texts (and, for that matter, paintings, furniture, and other products of human skill and imagination) depends very much on documented provenance. When it comes to books, particularly those published in the last 200 years, the book itself is its own documentation—a self-authenticator to those who know about books. There have been many forged books, but important forgeries have almost always been exposed—the vast majority of books are demonstrably what they say they are. Even more importantly, once authenticated, books remain the same. That attribute—fixity—when combined with the elaborate structures of writing, editing, publishing, bookselling, and reviewing, has led to an environment of trust and dependability that envelops author, reader, and scholar. Those who foresee the replacement of books by digital networks would do well to ponder the implications of such a shift, including the highly likely destruction of the environment of authenticity that has allowed scholarship and learning to flourish. There is a reason why plagiarism is the deadliest sin of all in the world of learning—it is the ultimate betrayal of the trust that is the vital element of scholarship. If a piece of writing is not what it says it is, how can it be studied and used to generate new knowledge? Gentle reader, if you have come this far in this little book, you will have done so in the sure knowledge that its ideas and theories (such as they are) are mine and if, as is quite possible, I am unknown to you, you do know that ALA Editions says that I am the author and their imprint on this book is a guarantee of that fact. If this or any other reputable publisher says that a book is by a particular author, you can bet your bottom dollar it is. Furthermore, this or any other book picked up in twenty years' time will have the same content that it has today.

None of these things are true about electronic resources and documents. You do not know if an electronic something that purports to be by Oliver Onions is by him. You have no publisher to certify that fact. Worse, you have no certain knowledge that the content of the resource or document is (*a*) truthful or (*b*) what it was yesterday and will be tomorrow. This mutability parallels that of the Manuscript Age, when written works were laboriously copied by hand. At that time, manuscripts could be added to, copied with alterations, destroyed, substituted by entirely different texts, and generally rendered untrustworthy. There is a whole branch of scholarship devoted to the authentication of manuscripts, which in turn is the necessary precondition for scholarly inquiry into their content. Digital documents and resources are even more fragile and mutable than manuscripts. Digital technology enables us to make undetectable and massive changes to documents and resources. The technology almost promotes such change, inviting the reader to interact with the author in ways that may promote new creativity but sabotage the message and intent of the original author. Here is something I found at irishmusicweb.ie:

Michael Gorman 1895–1970

Michael Gorman was born in County Sligo in 1895. He lived first in Doocastle, and then Achonry. His mother, Anne McGibbon, was a singer from Kilburn and his father, a small farmer, played the flute, the bagpipes, and the melodeon. When he was young, he was taken care of by foster parents who sent him for fiddle lessons to James Gannon, who also taught Michael Coleman. Artie Shaw used to tell the story about the master and pupil when Gorman was aged about nine: "Gannon wrote out the tunes in his own system of notation on pieces of card. Slowly these cards piled up under Michael's bed and he still could not hitch onto the fiddle. One day Gannon asked him to play *The Green Mountain.* Of course he could not, and Gannon broke the fiddle across Michael's head. He still has the scar."

Discography

Michael Gorman, the Sligo Champion, A musical biography, by Reg Hall. Topic *Irish Jigs, Reels and Hornpipes,* Michael Gorman and Willie Clancy, *Folkways. She Moved through the Fair,* Michael Gorman and Van Morrison. Topic *Her Mantle So Green,* Margaret Barry and Michael Gorman. Topic *Irish Music in London Pubs,* Margaret Barry, Michael Gorman and others, Folkways. *Irish Night Out,* Margaret Barry, Michael Gorman, The Dubliners and others.

Given a warning, any aficionado of Irish music could spot the changes that I have made in the text, the omissions from the biography, and the insertion of an entirely fictitious album in the discography (all very quickly and with great ease). For most people, this transfer of an altered text from the Web to the printed page, if anything, lends a spurious air of authority to the text and obscures its inauthenticity. The essential point is that there is no evidence (other than the possession of somewhat arcane knowledge) that this text is anything other than factual and complete. Once we know about its alteration, all trust is gone and the very existence of Michael Gorman, the Sligo Champion, is brought into question. In a scholarly field, such doubts are fatal. In a practical field, how much trust can the average nonlegal person place in all the legal information that is available in such profusion on the Web?

The question of the authenticity of, and trust in, texts and images is vital to human progress. It must be resolved if electronic documents and resources are to take their full place in the emerging library. Perhaps there are technological solutions such as electronic "fingerprints" left with each alteration, though such schemes would seem to have insuperable difficulties in application. Perhaps we will evolve preservation techniques that preserve each manifestation of each worthwhile (that word again?) document. Whatever the answers may be, they must be formulated and implemented sooner rather than later—before original electronic documents are lost in even greater numbers and before the system of scholarship and the reliable transfer of useful information is completely undermined.

SELECTIVITY

Though electronic documents and resources have many inherent problems and disadvantages, they have the undeniable asset of ease of access and use. (Both, of course, are confined to those with the capability of such access and use. See "Exclusivity" below.) Human nature being what it is, we should not be surprised that the average undergraduate student will prefer almost any electronic resource to almost any printed source. One has to move from a chair to obtain the latter and, once found, one cannot cut and paste (except in the most literal sense) texts and images into a paper. Such transfer of texts and images is by no means impossible when using print sources, but it requires far more physical and intellectual labor, not to mention possible illegality. The most obvious parallel with this change in research habits is in the wide popularity of fast food. Almost everybody knows that the great majority of this food is a nutritional nightmare (particularly for the child citizens of Fast Food Nation).[5] Almost everybody knows that home-prepared food is tastier, cheaper, and better for you. The key points for many are none of these—they are speed and convenience. Even when library users know (which most do not) that there is better information and recorded knowledge to be found on the shelves rather than on the screen, they still prefer the latter. Moreover, such users appear to be unaware of the very considerable drawbacks of search engines and fail to realize the many problems with precision and recall in the results that search engines deliver.[6] I believe that we are in danger of desensitizing an entire generation of library users who increasingly have come to believe that searching for recorded knowledge and information is a haphazard process with unpredictable results. Furthermore, they believe that any results are acceptable, irrespective of whether there are better results not retrieved by the search engine or better results not available in digital form. Both are almost invariably the case.

As usual, the answer lies in knowledge. It is essential that librarians in all kinds of libraries establish strong, continuing formal and informal library instruction programs. Such programs should be centered on the two vital themes of (a) questioning the worth of what is retrieved from cyberspace by search engines, and (b) stressing the worth of recorded knowledge and information in print and other nonelectronic formats. Library instruction should be concerned with strategies for counterbalancing the great weaknesses of search engines, to the limited extent that those weaknesses can be overcome. Beyond that, it should stress the importance of critical thinking in evaluating the results of such searches. It should point library users to the many alternatives to search engines. It should direct users to print and other tangible collections, stressing the rewards that can be gained from putting a little more effort into the gathering of information. We should be highly conscious here of the principle of least effort, which states, essentially, that a system (or person) will either try to adapt to its environment or will try to change the environment to suit its needs, whichever is easier. A library user who perceives that the use of whatever electronic sources are initially presented is easier than continuing to search for better resources, *and* who does not perceive that the extra effort will be of any measurable benefit will, obviously, choose the former. The task is to persuade library users that in most cases the extra effort is valuable, and will produce measurably more valuable results. We should never tire of pointing out that only a small fraction of the world's recorded knowledge and information is, or ever will be, available in digital form. Furthermore, most scholarly literature and belles lettres are unsuitable for digitization and are best used as print on paper. None of this amounts to book worship, but merely reflects the commonsense view that different kinds of human communication are better in different formats and will remain so.

EXCLUSIVITY

To live in our world is to live with deep-rooted, fundamental inequities that favor the First World, the white, the affluent, the male, and the educated. The average middle-class white person in the First World lives a life that is unimaginable to 99 percent of those living elsewhere. In a famous, if not exactly datable, moment, a reporter asked the Mahatma, "Mr. Gandhi, what do you think of Western civilization?" to which the sage replied, "I think it would be a good idea." His aphorism was a sly dig at the arrogance and pretension of the West, especially in the context of the British oppression of India (after all, one of the West's great heroes—Winston Churchill—had described Gandhi as "a half-naked fakir"). Despite this, it is hard to deny that the West has not only achieved great prosperity for the bulk of its citizens, but has also made historic breakthroughs in technology and in scholarship, learning, literature, and the arts. At first glance, it would seem that the task ahead is to spread these benefits and ideas throughout the world, but one then runs straight into accusations of political and cultural imperialism. The latter accusation is sharpened by the way in which the lowest aspects of Western, and specifically American, mass culture have spread like viruses throughout the world. The economic, medical, literacy, and digital divides may remain vast between the developed countries and the rest of the world, but most of the latter's inhabitants have worn a slogan-imprinted T-shirt, heard of Arnold Schwarzenegger, drunk Coca-Cola, or eaten a Big Mac. They may know nothing of Shakespeare, Darwin, Monet, or Goethe, but they know who Madonna and Michael Jordan are. Perhaps the crisis in confidence in the West about our intellectual and artistic achievements contributes to our inability to "sell" the benign "high-culture" products of the West nearly as well as we sell our toxic "low-culture" creations.

There is a school of thought (generally, but not entirely, among those from outside First World ways of thinking) that sees the intellectual and artistic achievements of the West as stultifying and ripe to be challenged by other ways of being and doing. If we are going to protect and promote the texts that embody large swathes of Western civilization, we must at least consider alternative views. The Native American activist Russell Means wrote:

> I detest writing. The process itself epitomizes the European concept of "legitimate" thinking; what is written has an importance that is denied the spoken . . . It is one of the white world's ways of destroying the cultures of non-European peoples, the imposing of an abstraction over the spoken relationship of a people. It seems that the only way to communicate with the white world is through the dead, dry leaves of a book.[7]

In those countries that are the home of Western culture, such a view is difficult to understand by both the people of the book and the people of the byte. Their differences lie in the manner in which they believe texts should be disseminated and preserved, not in rejecting the very idea of textuality. Libraries, by definition, have no place in an exclusively oral society dominated by the shaman and the griot.

Another view at odds with the fundamental idea of learning built on established texts is one that takes the mutability discussed in the previous section as a positive attribute rather than a challenge. In this worldview, texts lose the qualities of fixity and authenticity that have characterized them for the past 500 years, and the electronic text embraces changeability as a dominant characteristic. The author vanishes and the "reader" deals with a river of text, ever flowing and ever changing on its eternal way to an unknowable destination. Libraries have no place in this world either, but this would be among the least of the problems that society would face if the unchangeable structures of learning were to be replaced by the river of flux.

If we embrace neither of these antitext views, we must address the contradictions in society that result in technology comforting the comfortable and increasing rather than lessening the divides between rich and poor, old and young, men and women, and one ethnic group and another. The digital divide (discussed in earlier chapters) is but one manifestation of these contradictions. Another, mentioned by Professor Rutenbeck, is the dominance of the English language in most areas of global life, not least in the Web. There are many dialects of English, of course, but the educated speakers of each have little problem in understanding the educated speakers of the others. In any event, American English is the dominant language of global technology. What this means, of course, is that only the educated elites in non-English-speaking countries can participate fully in the global digital network. Moreover, the overwhelmingly poor, illiterate, or semiliterate populations of developed countries are not only estranged from libraries and learning but also from modern communications technology. This is so because they lack access to computers, access to the reliable power supply computers require, the skills necessary to operate them with profit, and the ability to decode the messages they deliver.

There are many other manifestations of what Rutenbeck calls "exclusivity," but they are all about power and the lack of it, money and the lack of it, and education and the lack of it. Most librarians and most libraries have the will to assist in bridging these various divides but, more often than not, have to spend a great deal of energy in getting the means and the support to play a helpful role in the libraries where that help would be most useful.

VULNERABILITY

Computer hackers hack for a variety of reasons—economic, political, and because they can. They are rulers of a small universe and that mastery conveys power, even if they have none in the rest of their lives. So an Israeli schoolboy launches a virus that has a crippling, if temporary, effect on the operation of one of the largest global companies, rejoicing in his anonymous earth-circling power. An animal rights activist attacks the computer system of a vivisectionist cosmetics firm. The world seems full of vandals and people with a cause who use computer attacks to express themselves, display their cleverness, and cause trouble for the entities they dislike. The world has always contained such people, but the range of their activities has always been limited by physical geography, if nothing else. No longer—we inhabit a world of fragile interconnectivity; a galaxy of hundreds of millions of connected and mutually dependent corporate and personal entities. In short, we are vulnerable to an extent never known before in many aspects of our commercial and social life. Many workers in stores, corporations, and noncommercial entities can only operate when they are connected to the electronic systems used by those entities. For example, when the system is up, there is no need for a clerk at a checkout counter to know how to add and subtract. When the system is down, such people are as incapable of performing their jobs as calculating machines without batteries.

Most routine library operations are automated, and so productive work is dependent on the availability of the system. There are often no manual analogues of the automated system, no means of getting at the data imprisoned in a crashed system, and no way in which the library can continue to provide users with the services they need. Systems crash because of accidents, carelessness, inherent flaws, or malicious action. Apart from local irritation, none of this would matter much if it were not for global connectivity and interdependence. The latter is our state, however, and libraries are no more immune than any other entities to the effects of mistakes and deliberate hacking. There are many instances in which a library's computer system has been used by hackers as the gateway to the computer systems of the wider entity (local governments, firms, universities, etc.). Hackers' reasons for choosing the library system for this role are many. We want as many people as possible to use the library's system and make it as accessible as we can, thus increasing our vulnerability to attack. When your library's catalogue and other services are available via the Web in Bergen (Norway), Buenos Aires, and all points in between, the universe of potential bad actors is greatly increased.

Beyond the vulnerability of libraries' systems lies the vulnerability of their content. Interconnectivity brings us the nightmare of the destruction, silent alteration, and silent addition of data, a nightmare whose effects may not be understood for years. New computer viruses always seem to be one step ahead of virus protectors and, therefore, almost impossible to fend off. Rutenberg is quite correct in posing "vulnerability" as a major challenge, and we may well have to wait a long time for that vulnerability to be lessened by new technological solutions. Libraries can only do the obvious things, while avoiding "security" measures that lessen access without justification, and wait for solutions we can use to emerge from other parts of the global computer network.

SUPERFICIALITY

For many of the reasons outlined above, our interaction with the Internet is, as Rutenbeck puts it, overwhelmingly superficial. This is in great part due to the limitations of cyberspace itself. How can we have a deep interaction with documents and resources that we cannot find or cannot identify within the inhumanly large lists produced by search engines? Serious work with electronic documents and resources requires wheat that is nearly invisible in the blizzard of chaff summoned up by truly awful retrieval systems. In addition, computer systems are very good at storing, transmitting, and retrieving bits of information (data and brief, discrete packages of text and images). By its nature, information, as such, does not permit deep interaction. It is there to be read and used or read and discarded. Conversely, computer systems are terrible at retrieving recorded knowledge (since they are all ultimately based on free-text searching), even for the masochistic few who wish to engage in sustained reading on computer screens.

Beyond the problems posed by the intrinsic nature of electronic documents and systems, there is another issue that mirrors the development of past means of human communication. There is, almost inevitably, a phase in the early years of a new means of communication in which there are high hopes that it will be used for a variety of high-minded and intellectual endeavors. Remember when the radio was going to revolutionize higher education by bringing the finest minds from academia into every home? Similar claims have been and are being made for the Internet. Virtual universities with virtual libraries were *the* coming thing only a couple of years ago. Every person was to be his or her own publisher, thus bringing a new renaissance of learning and letters. The masses, however, behave completely predictably and with natural common sense. They use computers for things that bring them pleasure (games, chatting, viewing pornography) without too much exertion or that provide affordable and easily accessible services such as shopping from home for books, CDs, and DVDs. When most people surf the Web they are not interested in doing more than flitting from one site to another—in fact, acting superficially and happy to be doing so. There are physical reasons why one cannot become engrossed in anything requiring deep thought on a computer—eyestrain, extraneous visual stimulation, etc.—and why it is unlikely that most people will ever transcend superficiality in their interactions with digital documents and systems. Certainly, doing so would require entirely new technologies—not just enhancements to existing technologies—and since, by definition, we cannot know what they are, it seems fruitless to speculate on their nature and impact.

Another issue of concern to Professor Rutenbeck is the superficiality of the interactions between people using computer technology. Our shelves are full of the collected letters and diaries of the great and infamous, and wonderful reading they are too. Care went into their composition, and these carefully composed texts are a silent tribute to a technology—pen and ink on paper—that almost compelled seriousness and focus. The mere thought of collecting, editing, and publishing the e-mails, text messages, and web pages of someone is enough to show the inherent superficiality of the medium (even if we make such strides in preservation that we could actually collect these digital communications decades after they were created). If, in our catalogues, the uniform title "Letters" were to be replaced with "Random, Ungrammatical, Misspelled Utterances," it would not be because today's great minds are less literate and articulate than those of yesterday (though they may well be), but because of the casual, superficial nature of communication via e-mail and the rest. It is not the computer that is at fault, either—Dickens's novels would have been just as great if he had used a word processor instead of a pen and ink—it is the way that many computer applications encourage superficiality and discourage thought and consideration over time.

All five of the challenges discussed above arise from the nature of electronic communication and its inherent shortcomings. Some can be mitigated by librarians in libraries, some need concerted societal action, and some have no presently conceivable resolution. All of these challenges must be at the forefront of our minds as we work to create library services and programs for the future.

NOTES

1. Marilyn Deegan and Simon Tanner, *Digital Futures* (New York: Neal-Schuman, 2002), 58.
2. Jeff Rutenbeck, "The Five Great Challenges of the Digital Age," *Library Journal Netconnect* (fall 2000): 30–33.
3. Linton Weeks, "E-Books Not Exactly Flying off the Shelves," *Washington Post,* July 6, 2002, p. C1.
4. A "definitive text" of *Ulysses,* edited by Hans Walter Gabler, was published in 1977. It has been under almost continuous attack ever since.
5. Eric Schlosser, *Fast Food Nation: The Dark Side of the All-American Meal* (Boston: Houghton Mifflin, 2001).

6. The precision ratio is a measure of the relevance of documents retrieved in a search; the recall ratio measures the number of documents retrieved against the total number of relevant documents.

7. Quoted in Michael H. Harris et al., *Into the Future,* 2nd ed. (Greenwich, Conn.: Ablex, 1998), 100.

9 The Future of Libraries
A Research Agenda

THE CENTRAL THEME OF THIS BOOK IS THAT WE ARE NOT IN AN EPOCHAL, TRANSFOR-mational time, but that we are at an important point in the evolution of libraries. We must confront the future without hysteria or pessimism and create new libraries not only with a due regard for the lessons of the past and our enduring values, but also with a reasonable optimism about the future. Our situation demands both clarity and purpose. It also demands tactical and strategic think-ing. Each of these can only be achieved if they are based on facts and the ratio-nal approach. Those facts and that approach can only be derived from research. The great problem here is the ever-widening gulf between the people who work in libraries and those who teach in what used to be library schools. There was once a golden age when library schools in U.S. research universities—notably Chicago, Columbia, Illinois, and Berkeley—produced a body of research that directly benefited and influenced the course of American librarianship. Unfor-tunately, of those four schools, only one still exists (the others having commit-ted suicide or been assassinated), and even more unfortunately, the research that goes on in their successors is largely academic, information science-oriented, and without widespread practical application. The time has come for our pro-fession to marshal all its human and financial resources and embark on a program of serious, practically oriented research that will benefit all library users and will enable us to see the present clearly and plan for a productive and harmonious future.

Pure research combines the highest intellectual, artistic, and spiritual aspi-rations of humankind. There is beauty and something uniquely human in the spirit of inquiry that seeks knowledge for its own sake and sees the elegance and wonder of new ideas about the world we live in. It is that spirit that has been able to discern patterns in the universe that mirror patterns in the smallest particles of matter and, from that, seeks a greater theory of patterns and a grand unified theory of the universe. Just as we all understand and accept the difference between pure science and applied science (technology) or between science and engineering, we instinctively understand such a difference in our own field. In the social and human areas of inquiry (of which librarianship is one), we need inquiry for its own sake (bibliometrics being an example), but we need research with practical ends in mind even more. Any student of libraries and librarianship can see that librarians are pragmatic people seeking technologies and methods that are intensely practical and results- and service-oriented. In my mind, the ultimate question about research in librarianship is: "What can we study in the hope that its results will improve our libraries and help library users?"

I am a librarian and my work has always been rooted in libraries, their structures, and their service to library users. I am not an "information scientist"—and, to tell the truth, have always had trouble defining what information science is. That trouble begins with the word "information" itself. I would maintain that libraries have always been more concerned with recorded knowledge and belles lettres than they have been with what I understand as "information." My definition of "information" is restricted to data and short, discrete packages of text and images that can be used without reference to any wider context. Facts and figures about the demographics of Fresno are information, as is the kind of brief description of Fresno and its history and geography that you will find in ready-reference materials and guidebooks. A book on Fresno and its history contains information, to be sure, but it contains much more than that.

This may seem a narrow semantic argument, but it goes to the heart of all discussion on the topic of librarianship and information science and the demarcation between them. If "information" means what I believe it means, then the science that deals with it is concerned with only a minute fraction of librarianship and library service. If, on the other hand, "information" comprehends any recorded or unrecorded human communication by means of texts, images, sounds, and symbols, then it means everything and nothing. Under that definition, the aesthetic appreciation of Leonardo's *Virgin and Child* is subsumed in information science, as are musicology, cartography, textual analysis, literary criticism, tarot card reading, library cataloguing, and on and on. This may seem a reductio ad absurdum (or an *expansio ad absurdum*), but how else should we define "information science"? Is information science a narrow area of study—the successor to the documentation movement of the 1940s and 1950s? Is it merely librarianship in a technological guise, as Lloyd Houser maintains?[1] Is it the massive and wide-ranging study of all human communication I have just described? Or is it, perhaps, what my friend Ellen Crosby called it—"librarianship practiced by men"?[2]

These questions, which I have posed in one form or another for years, remain unanswered and I shall, perforce, confine myself to discussion that is devoted to resolving the real problems that confront libraries, librarians, and library users today. My agenda will, of necessity, neglect pure research and its elegant pursuit of knowledge for its own sake. This is not because I disdain pure knowledge but because I believe we have a sufficiency of very serious practical problems facing us and cannot afford to spend a great deal of time and effort on speculative inquiry. The topics I will address are not equal in importance, but they are all important to the future of libraries and learning.

THE PRESERVATION CONUNDRUM

There is no doubt in my mind that the major issue facing libraries today is that of the preservation and onward transmission of the human record. This task has been accepted, usually tacitly, by many generations of librarians. The fact is that we librarians and archivists, and we alone, are responsible for something that everyone now takes for granted—that each generation will know more than the preceding generation because useful knowledge has been recorded and preserved and can be the basis for the creation of new knowledge, which, in turn, is preserved and made available by librarians and archivists. This cycle may seem almost commonplace, but it should be remembered that the Age of Print may turn out to be an aberration in human history—a scant few centuries in which very few texts and images were lost and we used a commonplace technology (print on paper) to ensure that the people of the future know all that we know. This was not true of the Manuscript Age and it may not be true of the Digital Age unless we, as stewards of the human record, take appropriate measures.

What have we done to ensure preservation of the human record in the Print Age, and what are the lessons we can draw from that experience? The first important characteristic of the Print Age was a stable technology used within a powerful economic model. Humans printed texts and images on paper, made many copies of each document, and distributed them widely throughout the world. That process was run, in most instances, on the reasonable desire of authors, publishers, and booksellers to be recompensed for their labors. In addition, we have, in recent decades, developed a system of global bibliographic control, admittedly not faultless, so that the human record was not only preserved but could also be retrieved and shared globally. We lived in an age of fixity, authenticity, and stability—a time in which preservation and biblio-graphic control were two sides of the same coin. Now, in contemplating digital documents and resources, both preservation and cataloguing are in doubt and each is dealt with as if it were completely separate from the other.

When it comes to preservation, our first problem is posed by the fact that, in the Print Age, we relied on publishers to decide what was and was not worth-while. Once printed by a reputable publisher, a book or other document was deemed, ipso facto, to be worthy of preserving. This is by no means so in the digital arena. "Publication" no longer implies any editorial judgment or any sort of imprimatur. The orderly world of the creation, editing, publishing, selection, and preservation of books has been replaced by a vast, global town square with millions of people shouting over each other's voices. How are we to make any sense of this cacophony, recognize the worthwhile voices, and preserve their productions for future generations?

I believe that the answer lies in some innovative research—in particular, we need the enumeration and taxonomy of the Web discussed in chapter 5. Huge, inhuman numbers for electronic sites and documents are thrown around when discussing preservation and cataloguing, and they tend to depress rather than stimulate thought and discussion. In addition, phrases like "cataloguing the Web" have been used in a form of false egalitarianism that proposes that all elec-tronic documents and resources are equal. The result of gigantic numbers and semantic vagueness has been a sort of despair proclaiming that we will never be able to bring the products of the Digital Age under any recognizable form of bib-liographic control or preserve any substantial portion of the digital ocean. I propose that we embark on an enumeration and taxonomy of the Web that is aimed at identifying and isolating those documents and resources that are worth cataloguing and preserving. I would propose that we consider a number of vari-ables, including:

- Is the resource commercial or not?
- Is it derived from print, archival, and other tangible documents or not?
- Is the document or resource static, cumulative, or constantly changing?

There are other variables, of course, but that is the point of research. We can start with the variables I propose and add others as the examination of facts warrants.

The distinction between electronic documents and collections of docu-ments on the one hand and websites on the other is crucial, as is the relative mutability of the resource. We tend to think that the most important demarca-tion is that between electronic and nonelectronic documents. I believe that when it comes to the preservation and cataloguing of electronic documents we should make other distinctions. Many such documents and sites are by-products of print and other publishing industries and hence are analogous to books, journals, sound CDs, films, etc. In addition, many sites are digitized archives that are either complete (i.e., static) or cumulative—that is, though they change, the change is in the form of additions and not deletions. Such sites are, again, analogous to "traditional" resources. Websites with constantly changing content, on the other hand, have no parallel in the world of print. They are more like those curious structures one sees in the streets of Paris that are erected to have posters plastered on them. The posters change, become torn and overlaid with newer posters, and are removed and vandalized with graffiti, so that the content and visual effect differ from week to week. Only the site endures. Since the content is so unstable and shape-shifting and since websites, unlike the Parisian structures, can vanish overnight, they are difficult, if not impossible, to bring under bibliographic control and to preserve. A possibly heretical question occurs to me—does that matter? An enumeration of sites that gives an idea about their subject matter, their creators, and their life span is very different from the cataloguing and preservation of content to which we are accustomed, but it may be all that we can accomplish. Furthermore, it may be all that such changing content deserves. I put this forward merely as a hypothesis, and leave it to researchers to show us whether that hypothesis is correct or whether there is some enduring part of the human record on these changing and vanishing websites that we should strive to preserve.

CREATING AND MAINTAINING THE BIBLIOGRAPHIC CONTROL WEB

I have written in earlier chapters of the interaction between preservation and cataloguing and the need to resolve the many issues involved in defining those electronic materials that need to be preserved and, therefore, catalogued. Beyond that, we need to create and maintain a structure of bibliographic control that will ensure the preservation of the records we create as well as the documents and resources they represent. The starting point should be the grand idea of universal bibliographic control, first put forward more than a quarter of century ago, in which individual libraries, regions, and countries cooperate to produce and share records without redundancy.

Then there is the question of cataloguing and metadata. The latter is an ill-considered attempt to find some kind of "third way" between the desert of search engines and free-text searching and the grand architecture of bibliographic control that librarians have developed over the last 150 years. Metadata is the product of bibliographic alchemists seeking the philosopher's stone who offer us effective cataloguing without expense and effective access without controlled vocabularies. There are no such things, and the sooner these notions are disposed of the better. Instead of the sterile discussions and failed schemes of metadata, we need inquiry and undisputed facts—in short, good research.

This research should be devoted to developing an internationally agreed data set, a set of agreements on international controlled vocabulary databases, interfaces between the artificial language of classification and the "natural language" of subject headings, and a developed international MARC format. This research is a combination of research into framework formats, content formats, international exchange structures, and database management—and it needs above all to clarify the distinctions between the various elements of the international bibliographic control architecture. Just as good research could lead to an international grand plan for preservation, it can lead to a complementary grand plan for the bibliographic control of all documents, irrespective of format.

USE AND DISSEMINATION OF SCHOLARLY ARTICLES

When people speak and write about "the serials crisis," they are usually referring to the high and ever-increasing costs of scientific, technological, and medical (STM) journals. Although journals in other areas can be expensive, they seldom approach the gaudy heights attained by the profiteers who publish STM periodicals. This is a continuing problem and one that has unfairly penalized journals across the board. However, I believe there is an as yet dimly perceived crisis that may eventually prove to be fatal. This crisis may alter the face of our libraries forever. It is the failure of anyone to come up with an economic model for scholarly communication in an electronic age. Print journals work economically because of a model that dictates that libraries buy articles, irrespective of whether they are used. Every year we commit to paying large sums for collections of articles that common sense and bibliometric studies tell us are read by few people or no one at all. We pay these sums because those articles are bundled with other articles that are heavily read by comparison. History decides which articles are of enduring value and will be read and cited over many years. For every article of the latter type there are four others read only by the author and his friends and relations.

There is no reason at all for scholarly communication to follow this pattern now. Indeed, there is no reason for electronic journals to exist. In truth, the electronic journal is a metaphor, not a reality; it is a prime example of changing the technology without fundamental rethinking—the mortal sin of technological innovation. The rub comes, of course, in deciding which articles will be bought by distant readers. If all the articles now published were to be made available and accessible through electronic means, someone would have to pay for that availability and access. There are very few successful commercial enterprises whose business plan consists of paying to make items available for purchase in the sure and certain knowledge that only one in five of those items will ever bring in any money.

What can library researchers and librarians do about this impending implosion of the scholarly journal industry? There has been much loose talk about academic libraries turning into publishers or working in consortia with the rest of the academy to create a not-for-profit scholarly communication system. I am not the most ardent capitalist in the world, but I think that we should reach out to help scholarly journal publishers make the transition from being sellers of journals to sellers of articles. It is obvious that they are floundering around—caught in an age of contradictions—and would welcome solutions to their seemingly insoluble dilemmas. Others in the penumbra of serial publishing (vendors, bundlers, and the like) are equally baffled. They all know, deep down, that the jig is up and would welcome clarification. The serial publishing industry is one of the few that depends on the work of highly educated unpaid workers—the authors, reviewers, and editors—working for the love of scholarship, egotism, the pursuit of tenure, and other nonmonetary rewards. Surely they could be enlisted to create a new electronic system of scholarly communication based on the authorship, review, indexing, and dissemination of individual articles. Such a system would bring monetary rewards to the commercial entities that finance it and tenure, recognition, and gratification to the unpaid scholars who do the intellectual work.

I realize this is just one approach, and detailed research into scholarly communication might well yield others. However, any such proposal must take into account the fact that scholarly communication is not exempt from the usual constraints of the world and must be paid for one way or another.

READING IN A DIGITAL AGE

There is little doubt that we live in a time when literacy is in crisis. In the developed world, literacy rates (seen merely as the ability to read at a functional level) are very high. Though we worry about the relatively small percentage of our populations that cannot read, we pay little attention to the rise in aliteracy—those who can read but don't, or who only read, for example, tabloid newspapers. When literacy is seen, as I believe it should, as a lifelong process of becoming ever more literate, of engaging in the sustained reading of complex texts, we see that it is under threat. It is possible to argue, quite plausibly, that we are on the edge of a new Dark Age in which learning will be the pastime of an isolated few, documents will be as mutable and perishable as the manuscripts that preceded the Age of Print, and the habit of sustained reading will be an eccentricity. The threat to reading is not the mass illiteracy of the historical Dark Ages but the aliteracy of the masses rendered soporific by infotainment and mindless diversions. I suppose it is better to be aliterate than illiterate, but operationally it seems a distinction without a difference. It is certainly better to be well-housed, healthy, and comfortable than to be a medieval peasant, but is an underclass sedated by electronic diversions a major cultural and intellectual improvement over the oppressed underclasses of the past?

No matter where one stands on the question of the Information Age, computerization, and all the other controversial phenomena that interest us, surely we can all acknowledge that human beings learn in three ways and only three ways. We learn from experience—something we have been doing since there have been human beings; we learn from others who know more than we do (teachers, gurus, and the like); and we learn from interacting with the human record—something the mass of people have been doing for only the last two centuries. This third form of learning demands literacy. At the end of the day, a seeker of learning is presented with a text, and whether that text is on a screen or on paper is insignificant when compared to the reader's ability to understand, analyze, and absorb the meaning of that text. This whole issue, of course, is something that goes well beyond the traditional concerns of libraries, and one could argue that libraries and librarians should simply observe and wait to see how things turn out. I would suggest that we take a much more aggressive and activist stance, and would maintain that LIS schools and library researchers are very well positioned to form alliances with researchers in other fields to address this crucial issue.

Here are the questions that researchers should be asking:

What are the levels of higher literacy, functional literacy, aliteracy, and illiteracy in today's societies?

What is the effect of those levels on the learning process, education, and the use of libraries?

What can librarians do to encourage literacy and learning in academia, the schools, and society as a whole?

What would be the effects of a postliterate society on libraries?

COMPUTER TECHNOLOGY AND PUBLISHING

One of the paradoxes of the Computer Age is that the impact of computerization on print publishing has been almost the opposite of what might have been expected. It was widely forecast a decade ago that electronic text would supplant print. Raymond Kurzweil, to take but one instance, said that no printed books would be published by the year 2000.[3] In fact, book publishing in the United States and Europe is near or at all-time highs. To take two significant examples of how print and computerization have interacted in unexpected ways: computerization has made the production of high-quality books far cheaper than before; and the computerization of the production process makes the dissemination of texts in electronic form cheap and easy. Computerization has made the production of books and periodicals far cheaper and quicker by eliminating redundancies in the editorial and typesetting processes. The most obvious example of this is the free availability of newspapers from all over the world on the Internet. Far from supplanting books and journals, computerization is making the publishing process better and quicker and is making texts more available by the added value of Internet availability.

The rapid rise and, in the United States at least, fall of the e-book is a case in point. In 2002, the only credible American producer of e-books was reported to be on the verge of bankruptcy, had abandoned any idea of marketing its products to individuals, and was bailed out by OCLC. There is preliminary evidence that the use of e-books in libraries is concentrated on reference materials, computer manuals, and other texts that can be used for consultation rather than sustained reading.[4] Another interesting phenomenon is the case of the National Academy Press, which has made all its publications (2,100 books, 400,000 book pages) available on the Internet free of charge to anyone who wants them.[5] The salient point of this story is that the sale of the press's printed books has *increased* since it adopted the free distribution of their electronic analogues. It is not just the print publishing industry that has had to face the challenges and opportunities of computerization. The Napster controversy over the production and distribution of sound recordings is just the best-known example in the nonprint world. Technology made a system of organized theft of intellectual property (in the case of Napster, sound recordings) possible and no one has found a satisfactory way of curbing this aural crime wave.

It is clear that there is a pressing need for hard research in this area. What is the potential role, if any, of the pure e-book? How has print publishing been changed by computerization? Which printed texts could migrate completely to electronic forms? What is the economic model for the hybrid print/electronic publishing industry of the future? What is the economic model for the web-based distribution of sound recordings, films, and other nonprint works? How can intellectual property rights be safeguarded in an age that is as advanced technologically as it is backward morally?

THE LIBRARY SERVICES GAP

I will write here only of the situation in the United States. I have written earlier of the "digital divide"—the fact that wealthier urban people are more likely to have access to information technology than poorer rural people. Though the media and politicians have concentrated on this fact alone, it is merely one aspect of a much longer-lived and more enduring phenomenon. The fact is that if you are an American who is old, young, poor, physically or mentally handicapped, a member of an ethnic minority, or live in a rural area, you will not have as good access to library services as those who fall into none of these categories. It may be unfortunate to be a young person without access to information technology, but how much worse it is to be a young person who can barely read, who attends a school without a library, and lives in a place without a public library. The chances of that young person ever becoming an educated, empowered individual approach zero, and giving him or her access to a computer is unlikely to improve those chances. What we need are good hard figures on the "library services divide," and these, when supplemented by the detailed research into literacy that I mentioned before, would at least give us a map of the problem and would suggest means to overcome it. No one needs research to tell them that the "library services divide" is rooted in disparities of funding between, for example, suburban and inner-city schools, but we do need research that demonstrates the effects of those disparities and indicates the areas to which whatever funds are available should be directed.

LIBRARY EDUCATION AND "CORE COMPETENCES"

Library education in the United States is approaching a catastrophe. Even those who take a more benign point of view acknowledge that we have problems. This recognition prompted the American Library Association to hold two national conferences, one on educating would-be librarians and the other on continuing education. The first conference gave rise to two task forces. One was on the "core values" of the profession—a matter that remains officially under discussion despite the fact that the first statement crashed and burned in the ALA Council. The second was on "core competences." There seems to be general agreement that there is a gap between what LIS schools teach their students and what libraries require of new employees. The gap is not new but its evolution into a gulf is. As recently as twenty years ago, most librarians and library educators would have agreed that a newly graduated librarian should know about reference work, collection development, cataloguing, library automation, one particular kind of librarianship (academic, public, children's, etc.), and administration. There may have been disputes about the penumbra of courses around those basic topics. Systems? Bookbinding? Storytelling? There may even have been topics that were perceived as central at one time but later fell out of favor. The "library hand" and tachygraphy were core courses in Melvil Dewey's time, computer programming was a mandatory course in some library schools a couple of decades back, and today topics like Java script and web page design are deemed essential by many. However that may be, reference and other traditional core topics featured in all library education until the past decade. I recently met a very bright graduate of an ALA-accredited "school of information" who had only received an introductory reference course and had never taken a cataloguing course en route to obtaining her master's degree.

That such a shameful state of affairs can exist is not entirely the fault of the "information scientists" who infest the American LIS schools. It can also be attributed to the lethargy and indifference of those who employ those schools' graduates—the people who run academic and other libraries. Even those administrators who have eviscerated their cataloguing departments must be aware that effective reference service is at least partly dependent on knowing how recorded knowledge and information are organized and retrieved. Lacking such knowledge, how is a reference librarian to guide and assist library users who know there must be something more to life than search engines? Lacking such knowledge, how can anyone be an effective library instructor or a teacher of information competence? Lacking such knowledge, how can anyone construct and implement effective collection development plans? Also, what about those eviscerated cataloguing departments? The enormously successful global bibliographic control system of the past decades owes its very existence to contributions from cataloguers in libraries great and small, general and specialized. Are we to abandon that achievement in a spectacular exhibition of penny wisdom and pound foolishness?

Perhaps we will stagger toward oblivion blaming today's LIS schools for the dearth of useful, educated employees while they enjoy the death of a profession for which many of them have little regard. Perhaps not. Perhaps we will embark on an endeavor to define the skills needed by a modern librarian and rebuild our profession on that definition. It seems obvious to me that task forces and the like cannot do that work without detailed facts and understanding of the realities of modern library work. I could draw up a list of what I think a librarian should know, and so could any of you, but neither would be rooted in anything but our experience and view of libraries. I think we need hard research and detailed observations, not just of what is happening in our libraries today, but also of the services that our users need and desire and may or may not be getting. Armed with the fruits of such research, we could possibly unite librarians and library educators around a common definition of our profession in the twenty-first century.

We stand, then, at a point in history when the profession of librarianship can either rise to even greater heights or descend into a fractious and incoherent dissolution with grave consequences for our culture and society. If we are to achieve the former and avoid the latter, we need to look with clear eyes at our present situation and future prospects. The clear eyes we need are those of researchers—those who pursue the truth without bias and shine a light on our misconceptions and follies as well as our value and values.

NOTES

1. Lloyd Houser, "A Conceptual Analysis of Information Science," *Library and Information Science Research* 10 (January 1988): 3–34.

2. Quoted in Michael Gorman, "A Bogus and Dismal Science," *American Libraries* (May 1990).

3. Raymond Kurzweil, "The Futurecast: The Future of Libraries," pts. 1–4, *Library Journal* (1991–92), vol. 117, no. 1, p. 81; no. 3, p. 140; no. 5, p. 63; vol. 118, no. 3, p. 145.

4. Stephen Sottong, "E.book Technology: Waiting for the 'False Pretender,'" *Information Technology and Libraries* 20, no. 2 (June 2001): 72–80.

5. Michael Jensen, "Academic Press Gives Away Its Secret of Success," *Chronicle of Higher Education* (September 14, 2001): 24.

10 Information Overload and Stress
The Ailments of Modern Living

THE AVALANCHE OF INFORMATION

It is 10 p.m.—do you know where your mind is tonight? Your day started when you rose early to check your e-mail at home, your cell phone for voice mail and text messages, your fax machine for overnights, and newspapers on the Web for news and other texts and pictures. Breakfast was accompanied by the local newspaper and radio news or an early morning television show. On the television, you saw not only pictures of the host and guests with text identifying each as they appeared, those appearances being punctuated with advertisements containing images, text, and sound, but also a small box showing a live event, and a "crawl" of "breaking news" and news snippets. Then it was time to leave for work, the commute being accompanied by more reading on the train or bus, not to mention consulting and updating your PDA; or more spoken words on the car radio or audiotape player, interrupted by calls on your cell phone. By the time you actually reached the library in which you work, you had already read more words, seen more images, and heard more music and spoken words than you could possibly absorb and process. At the library, there were the usual memoranda, e-mail messages, faxes, voice mail messages, post-it notes and other handwritten messages, professional journals and newsletters, meetings, and conversations—a never-ending stream of communications of all kinds. All of these are supposed to support your working life and private life and to assist you as you go about the tasks for which, at least in theory, you are paid—administration, cataloguing, reference work, library instruction, etc. At the end of the workday, you returned home, in all probability to deal with yet more communication. More messages invade your private life from the television, chat shows

122

on the radio (the natural habitat of the ignorant in possession of random information they are incapable of integrating), the Web on your home computer, magazines, manuals, and more e-mails and faxes. Perhaps you are like the journalist William Van Winkle, who "gets antsy after a single day without checking" his e-mail and confesses "[a]t night, I read constantly from the dozen or so periodicals to which I subscribe while my wife channel surfs. This is our relaxation time?"[1]

I suspect most librarians imagine an ideal evening of leisure as being some variation on the home life of Inspector Morse—the easy chair, opera on the stereo, cryptic crossword puzzles, the classic novel or literary biography, the snifter of Armagnac within convenient reach—the whole civilized, gently lit pattern of the life of the mind. How different the reality—the unread books and magazines, ever-present television chatter and noise, the e-mails and the fax messages, yakkers on cell phones in places public and private, the flood of unread or unabsorbed messages bombarding us all our waking hours. Worse, all of these media are open to ever-present abuse. Take, for example, the junk e-mail popularly known as "spam." We are all deluged with these unwanted and irrelevant assaults on our privacy. The syndicated columnist Ellen Goodman writes that today 11 percent of all e-mail messages are spam; that the average e-mail user received 1,470 "unsolicited commercial messages" in 2001; and that number will rise to 3,800 in 2005.[2] Among the other data and information intrusions that cost the advertisers little or nothing but cost us time and cause us stress are telemarketers, fax advertisements, pop-up ads on websites, the exploitation of "cookies," nearby cell phone users, junk mail, and those little cards that fall like snowflakes from magazines. The result of this ever-flowing river of information, noninformation, and misinformation is a state of inadequacy and stress that can only be ameliorated by drastic measures most of us are incapable of carrying out.

The blight from which we suffer is called "information overload"—the end result of a society in which technologies have outstripped the ability of the human brain to deal with their importunities. Writing on a web news site, Paul Krill tells us that information overload "results from having a rapid rate of growth in the amount of information available, while days remain 24 hours long and our brains remain in roughly the same state of development as they were when cavemen communicated by scrawling messages on stones."[3]

Speaking of the human brain, this might be a good point to examine what "information" is in the context of our ability to process it. Charles Jonscher imagines a Neolithic hunter-gatherer of ten millennia ago, alert in his lonely, pristine surroundings, taking in all the signals that he receives from his surroundings by looking. "In short, with this brief scan of the horizon, the hunter-gatherer's eyes receive *data,* his optic nerves and visual cortex process it into *information,* his brain's cerebellum makes it into *knowledge.*"[4] This neural analysis is most helpful in addressing the issues of information overload. We receive the data—the random messages from the world around us, some natural, some shaped by a human mind—and try to process them into information and, in so doing, become informed. That process, of course, involves selection and rejection and ranking in terms of importance—often at great speed. In a world where the latter activities are virtually impossible, what hope is there for us in attempting to employ our cerebral cortex (the part of the brain in which profound thinking takes place) to transform that information into knowledge? Charles Jonscher defines knowledge as "something deeper and more lasting, the body of things known."[5] It is there that the exhausting and demoralizing nature of information overload is made manifest. We know we should be making more of all the data and messages that we receive, but their sheer volume, randomness, lack of organization, and febrile quality make it impossible for us to do just that. Anyone who has ever taken a block of time off from the "information age" and devoted that time to reading a good book knows the satisfaction that comes from adding to one's knowledge from an organized and authentic source. At such times, even the least of us can glimpse wisdom and can profit from the immortality of the human record.

Information overload is more than an annoyance and worse than difficult to deal with. It can be dangerous to your mental and physical health. David Schenk analyzed a variety of writings on stress caused by information and stimulus overload and came up with an alarming list of their effects.[6]

Increased cardiovascular stress. This is caused by a rise in blood pressure resulting from ever-more futile attempts to deal with information overload.

Weakened vision. It is widely known that the increasing use of televisions, computer screens, and other visual information display devices is leading to an epidemic of shortsightedness and other visual problems.

Confusion. An excess of shallowly processed information and the inability to rank and give priority to that information inevitably leads to confusion of mind.

Frustration. This is a natural reaction to the inability to deal with all the messages and to reach the seemingly unattainable goal of integrated and assimilated information—of being in charge. Such information powerlessness often leads to anger born of frustration, a mortal enemy of good decisions and a harmonious and healthy life.

Impaired judgment. Schenk quotes psychologists (Siegfried Streufert and others) as writing that, after a certain point, the flow of information decreases the ability to make good decisions. If all necessary information cannot be absorbed and deployed, how can informed decisions be made?

Decreased benevolence. Studies show that people under stress because of information overload become, essentially, self-centered and unempathetic. This is certainly the case for those (especially young people) exposed to excessive infotainment stimuli.

Overconfidence. People suffering from information overload often fail to realize their situation and become overconfident, thinking that they have been empowered by unprocessed information when the opposite is the case.

I would add *resignation* and *despair* to Schenk's list of woes brought on by information overload. We can see many library users resigned to being unable to deal with, for example, thousands of results from a simple search and settling for something—anything—from that pile. Most of us have experienced the first flickering of the deadly sin of despair when confronted with more information and messages than we can deal with, and some may even have succumbed to despair—or, as it is now called, burnout.

So what should we do? In our daily work, most librarians cannot retreat to that house in the country with no computer or television; we cannot ignore the messages that make up so much of the work that we do. Just think of what happens on the days, or more likely, the hours when the library's system is down for one reason or another. Neither you nor your coworkers heave a grateful sigh and turn to the delights of penmanship and the good book read at leisure. The more likely reaction is one of increased stress and anxiety, of nervousness and frantic phone calls. We feel that, without the network and system, working life lacks zest and, dare we say it, *authenticity* if we are not continuously in touch, switched on, wired, and living at the level of real-time messages. The term "real time" is, in itself, most interesting. In the context of human communication, "real time" equals "simultaneous" and is a most telling term because it equates "instantaneous" with real, and, by inference, "delayed" with unreal. The idea that something read and absorbed over time is inferior to something that is perused, and probably forgotten, in an instant is deeply flawed and deeply injurious. The life of the mind is not lived in "real time"—it is lived in thought, rumination, and incorporation over those weeks, months, and years that presumably constitute "unreal time."

What should we do, as librarians, to deal with the information overload (and concomitant knowledge deficit) that is our lot today? The following are some rules and suggestions.

Avoid electronic discussion lists and newsgroups. One of the claims of those who promote the Web and the "information society" is that they enable an individual to converse and interact with others across the world. At one level, this is true. You *can* be in touch with people all over the country and the world, but after experience with many electronic discussion lists and newsgroups, do you *want* to be in touch? I was, for a while, a member of a discussion list dedicated, in theory, to an important professional topic—intellectual freedom—because I had a committee assignment that made it necessary for me to be aware of developments in that area. The list was populated and dominated by a handful of people (significantly, most sailing under adolescent pseudonyms) whom it would be polite to describe as cranks and egomaniacs. Petty quarrels abounded, "threads" of especial inanity were pursued with solipsistic intensity, and the general effect was of swimming in a tiny fishbowl that provided the ideal venue for people who would never be big fish except in their imaginations. As most people who have experience with discussion lists can attest, this was not, unfortunately, an aberrant list. Even the more worthy discussion lists (e.g., the ALA Council list and AUTOCAT) suffer from giganticism, and the press of the flood of messages is ultimately wearing and wearying. The best solution is to unsubscribe and to cultivate friends who do monitor the list in which you are interested and can be counted on to forward any item of interest (especially those that mention your name). The second best solution is to sever your ties with discussion lists altogether. You will miss very little and that little, if it is important, will wend its way to you eventually.

Avoid meetings. As Oscar Wilde observed, "work is the curse of the drinking classes." Meetings are the curse of the library world. Fueled by theories about participation, egalitarianism, and the cult of "the team," meetings have grown in number and in length, and the amount of time devoted to them has expanded at the expense of time devoted to real work. Your strategies as a librarian dealing with the problem of meetings will differ depending on your status in the library. If you are in charge, you have the power to limit the number of meetings, ensure that those meetings that do take place stay with the agenda and are focused on outcomes, and make the meetings end on time. Above all, apply Occam's razor and stop meetings from multiplying beyond the necessity for them. If you are a junior member of the library, you have no such control except over your own behavior. Even in that relatively powerless position, there are positive things to be done. Do not be a bloviator. Speak concisely and to the point. Ask pertinent questions that can shorten the meeting. Speak truth to power. Note carefully those things that you will change someday when you are running meetings.

Have and stick to priorities. The fog of messages can easily obscure your priorities and may even make it difficult for you to formulate those priorities. Various messages implying or necessitating action can cancel each other out and lead to a kind of paralysis if they are not assigned priorities. A few pauses spent in thought each week, when you formulate short lists of what you want to achieve, can be most refreshing and helpful. If you are a cataloguer, decide how many and which kinds of materials you want to catalogue in the next few days and which events and processes are likely to interfere with that cataloguing. If you are a reference librarian, decide what the focus of your activities over the next few days will be. For example, decide how much time you need to prepare for library instruction classes, how to approach your desk time, which barriers to harmony in your work need to be overcome and which should be ignored. If you are a children's librarian, ensure that time available for interaction with the children is not encroached upon by tasks or obligations of lesser importance. No matter which part of librarianship or type of library you are devoted to, decide what is important and what takes precedence and allow that decision to guide your working life.

Have a wider vision. It is easy to blunder about in the fog of data and to become consumed with the trivial and evanescent. How many of us pause to think what our library is about and why being a librarian is important? Despite appearances and our protestations, it is our inability to deal with the barrage of data and information to which we are subjected and not just the press of work that prevents us from taking such a pause. Information overload is the enemy of vision and the broad view, and since we all perish without a vision, we have to deal with the overload issue if we are to function in a healthy and productive manner.

Take breaks from work and communications. This obvious advice is made more difficult by modern technology. I confess that I travel with a laptop that I use for e-mail and a cell phone with which I call my office. Moreover, I am writing this at home on a Sunday afternoon after having checked my e-mail several times today and having used the Web to dig up some facts for this book. All this being said, I would be happier and you would be happier if we could disengage from all this communication on weekends or on frequent short breaks and, certainly, when taking longer vacations. Many years ago, I knew a librarian who ran a branch of a public library and was advised to take a cruise to "get away" from the stress of her job. She was relaxing in a deck chair with a book on the first day out when she was joined by a patron of her library who proceeded to complain at great length about many of the library's services. They were seven days from the next port and his complaints went on for all those days. That was nearly forty years ago. Today, my poor librarian would not only be plagued by the importunate user but would also be the recipient of messages from her library all day. It would take nimbleness and a great effort of will to escape from it all. However, most of us are not stranded on boats and can exercise choice. As Peter Drucker implies, not being able to get away from your job is a sign of a half-lived life, and often betrays an unhealthy level of insecurity rather than a lack of dedication.

> The effective people I know simply discipline themselves to have enough time for thinking. Maybe it is a few hours or a few weeks in the summer, or by locking the door and disconnecting the phone for three hours. Being on the job—except in an emergency—24 hours a day simply means you are incompetent.[7]

The best course (and how much I wish I had the strength of mind to follow it) is to take breaks of various lengths, both from your work and from messages. I have no scientific evidence to support this, but I would bet my last dollar that someone who eats at her desk while working is ultimately less productive than someone who takes a lunch break from work and converses (on topics other than work) or reads a book while eating. Surely the latter individual will be better off psychologically and physiologically, in which case the library and its users will be better off too.

Avoid self-sacrifice. My late father, a career soldier, used to say the motto of the British Army should be "Look out for Number One"—that is, your first duty is to yourself. The line between enlightened self-interest and pure selfishness is, as we all know, often difficult to draw, especially for librarians. We tend to be service-oriented and, if not exactly conforming to the Buddhist ideal of "selfless persons," we tend toward self-sacrificing actions.[8] I don't think we can afford this stance in the face of the pressures of modern technology and economics.

Frankly, I believe that librarians should be more self-interested than many are and should also recognize that their self-sacrificing behavior can have adverse effects on themselves and their colleagues. A decent regard for our own interests should be applied to the choices we make at work, and the extent that work impinges on our private lives. I know a large number of librarians who work brutally long hours without additional recompense because of the way they perceive the necessities and demands of their work. This is noble and admirable insofar as it is dedicated to service to library patrons, but inevitably self-defeating when it comes to its impact on colleagues and successors. Let me state it baldly. A library administration or governing board that relies on selfless dedication to make up for the underfunding of essential services is, wittingly or unwittingly, exploiting the very qualities that make a good librarian. Just think of the successor to such a person who hears, early in her tenure, "Oh, going home at 5? Linda always used to work until 7:30 to make up for the time when there is no librarian to work the desk." Work life is full of these small social and peer pressures and we dismiss them at our peril. Just as we should balance our work and private lives in our own self-interest, we should exercise that same self-interest in dealing with information overload. A voice on voice mail is not a message from on high that must be responded to immediately, nor is a fax marked "URGENT" necessarily so. Some steel in the backbone is required but you should never allow yourself to be stampeded by the importunity of the messages that are spawned by modern technology.

Learn to say "No." This injunction is a natural spin-off of the injunction to "avoid self-sacrifice." It arises from the pressures of technology and of the economic state of libraries. Technology, considered separately, imposes pressures because of its impression of urgency, but those pressures are quite small when compared with the pressures that have arisen because, in almost all libraries, technology has been added to other services and has almost never displaced those services. Invitations to be on time-consuming task forces with no clear outcome, to attend meetings that are of peripheral interest, or to participate in continuing e-mail discussions on almost any topic should be resisted. They all involve time taken from your primary task and they all dilute your energies. A focused librarian doing cataloguing, reference work, library instruction, or collection development with energy not depleted by trivial pursuits is likely to be better at those tasks and to be a happier person.

Do not distribute your home phone number, individual (not office) work number, fax number, and e-mail address widely. When the inventor of voice mail, Gordon Matthews, died in February 2002, every obituary and every commentary contained a reference to the unintended consequences of technological innovation, something of which Matthews was well aware. He was fond of saying, "Half the world loves me, and half the world hates me." To quote one obituary, "Before Matthews came along, you could actually connect with a real live person when you called a company instead of being consigned to voice mail purgatory."[9] It was, to be fair, not Matthews's fault that companies took an idea that was intended to make it easier for human beings to communicate and turned it into an inhuman struggle between increasingly angry people and implacable machines. However, the fact remains that voice mail is merely one of the technological innovations in communication that were meant to improve our lives and have ended up creating new levels of tension and frustration.

I am convinced that the reason many people consult their e-mail, call in to their voice mail, and use their PDAs even when on vacation is that they cannot bear the idea of what will await them when they return to two or three weeks' worth of accumulated messages. Such use of communications technology is driven by fear more than obsessiveness and the idea that staying wired every day is better than being buried by an avalanche of panic-inducing messages upon returning to work. These are, to a great extent, inevitable problems in today's libraries, but they can be mitigated if you are sparing in disseminating e-mail addresses, fax numbers, private phone numbers, and other cyberlocations any more than is absolutely necessary.

Find time for informal discussions. Meetings more often blight than illumi- nate. Unfortunately, they may be the only occasion for human interaction in the modern library (and the modern workplace in general). I think it very impor- tant that the working day afford time for informal discussion between colleagues in which they can cut through the haze of information overload and speak about more than the problems of the moment or the latest facts and information. The trick, of course, is to have working environments that encourage such interac- tions but do not force them on the unwilling or add more stress to the stressed.

Concentrate on your real job. Many ill-digested management theories have been welcomed into libraries in the last two decades. (The fact that they are mostly half-baked to begin with has not helped the digestive process.) One theory that has had many negative consequences centers on the concept of "teams" (under this or other names). There are many manifestations of this basic idea, some derived from sports analogies and others from the methods of Japanese manufacturing companies. It is hard to imagine how anyone ever thought that either of these milieus had anything of value to offer to the running of libraries, but there we are. People did and we all suffered. In most areas of intellectual life, it is the individual mind—that of the author, teacher, composer, painter, reference librarian, or cataloguer—that is important. When collabora- tion is common (as, for example, with composers and lyricists), it is usually manifest in people with complementary skills working together rather than people with roughly the same skills forming some robotic, goal-oriented sum that is greater than its parts. The latter may work in the manufacture of Nissan cars or in success on the football field, but it has been shown to have little or no relevance to the majority of library tasks. Still, administrative careers have been built on the application of management fads, with cataloguing departments giving way to "bibliographic access teams" and reference libraries to "interpre- tative services task forces." Fads come and go and maybe these names are merely silly, but I believe that this movement has not only devalued individuality but has also led to a serious lack of clarity and focus in the lives of many working librarians. In turn, this lack of clarity and focus, when combined with information overload, has added stress to many working lives. It is imperative that every librarian understands clearly what his or her main job is. How else can he or she assign priorities and make intelligent choices when confronted with sixty hours of work in a forty-hour workweek? No one should be forced to abdicate the main purposes of his or her working life in favor of a slushy mess of "teamwork" and other anti-humanist concepts.

Never "surf the Web." This is a deceptively simple instruction that is devilishly difficult to obey. I suppose when web surfing is purely recreational it is relatively harmless, though time spent reading, knitting, tap-dancing, or almost anything else would be far better for the mind and body. The real danger is when an ostensibly work-related activity leads one into the infinite electronic hall of mirrors. More and more librarians (and others) turn to the Web for information and find that they are adding to their information overload. The quest begins with a desire to solve something and move on, but it ends with more questions and few answers. This is not true for a minority of strong-minded people who can access the Web; find a text, image, or factoid speedily; and leave the Web with dispatch. They are today's version of those who, in the days when we used to smoke, could enjoy a cigarette on special occasions and eschew them for the rest of the time. Most of us are always in danger of contracting a 100-website-a-day habit and, once enticed into entering the dark forest, become beguiled as we are led deeper and deeper into it, entranced by the shifting shapes and the world of things that are not what they seem. In the end, web-surfing is not only a useless activity but also something that makes information overload worse.

Get a hobby and devote time to it. The trend today is toward hobbies that focus on physical activities. Stamp collecting, train spotting (not a fruitful occupation in contemporary America), and chess have yielded to aerobics, spandex-clad cycling, and rock climbing. I have a predilection for more cerebral activities (but that is because I am unsuited to strenuous physicality in almost every way), but either sphere offers what is needed—a focused escape from the stress of information overload. Losing oneself in genealogy or fly-fishing is a wonderful way to achieve balance in a world of nervous workaholics. Family, libraries, and outside interests are the three areas that every librarian has to balance. Library work and the information overload it generates should never be allowed to be negative influences on the other two areas.

Eschew trends and resist peer pressure. Librarians work in a world where lazy clichés like "the information age" and "legacy collections" ("books" to you and me) are the common currency of conversation. Library administrations (especially those in large libraries) are peculiarly prone to fall for the illusions of neophilia and the idea that this is a uniquely transformational age. This leads to the embrace of the management fads of the moment—usually at least two removes from the corporate culture in which they originate. It also leads to skewed priorities, as large sums of money are spent on resources for the benefit of a minority of library users at the expense of majority tastes and preferences. Both the pressure from above to follow the party line and the pressure from peers to be a conformist arise partly from the inability of administrators and colleagues to take a step away from the information overload with which they cannot deal. These are times when taking a step back from the trees and considering the forest are the most useful abilities a librarian can possess. It is hard to combat such pressures (and impossible if burdened with information overload), but doing so may well represent a significant contribution to library service and the library's users.

Meditate. There is ample written evidence that for those with the skills and training, meditation has great value for mental and emotional health.[10] It is the perfect antidote for information overload because the desired outcome is a clearing of the mind and escape from the stress of the trivial and mundane. Even those without the skills or the aptitude for meditation as such can benefit from periods of quiet contemplation, of removal from the barrage of messages, and of concentration on the important things about work and life. Some would say they have not the time for such meditation or reflection, but I would say that one cannot afford not to spend that time in such a useful and beneficial manner.

Make time to read. This is the simplest, most rewarding, and most effective of these precautionary injunctions. In the interview I cited earlier, Peter Drucker was asked, "What do you think today's leading-edge knowledge worker should be reading?" He answered:

> The important thing is that he or she should be reading. They'll need continuing education in their specialty. Knowledge changes incredibly fast . . . That is the greatest difference between skills and knowledge. Skills historically changed very slowly . . . the first thing for the knowledge worker is to keep on reading to keep abreast of his or her knowledge area.[11]

This might be called the utilitarian basis for continuing reading as the best means to keep up with one's field. Though this is undoubtedly important and, in areas subject to great change, vital, it is only one facet of the benefits of reading. It is often said that there is no difference in the act of reading caused by the format in which the text is presented. This is correct from a mechanical point of view (if a computer screen that is "just as good as a book" is ever perfected), but it ignores the different nature of the texts presented. Journal articles, even those published in prestigious literary and learned journals, often represent the first thoughts of the author on but one aspect of his or her life's work or preoccupation. Books, from reputable publishers, embody the considered and complete ideas and thoughts of their authors. The journal article can be seen as the first draft of part of the subsequent book. That being so, how much earlier in the evolution of ideas and thoughts are most of the texts found on the Internet? (I exclude, of course, those electronic documents that are derived from print.) The medium is not the message, but the content of texts is inevitably influenced by the medium in which those texts are presented. In general, the reading of books is indisputably an activity of higher intellectuality than the reading of journal articles, which is, in turn, a more valuable way of spending time than the reading of random electronic documents. Quite apart from the value of the content of books, there is the opportunity they afford for contemplation and escape. "Escapist literature" is generally considered to be descriptive of the mindless ephemera that occupy four-fifths of the *New York Times* bestseller list, but the true escape is to be found in works of the imagination and nonfiction that engage and expand the mind, imparting insights that transmute knowledge into understanding. In reading these books, one escapes from the depressing world of information overload into the uplifting worlds of the life of the mind and the imagination. In this way, reading is not only therapeutic but also, to use a very old-fashioned word denoting an even more old-fashioned concept, improving. To adapt the words of the philosopher Timothy Leary—read on, tune in, drop out of information overload.

NOTES

1. William Van Winkle, "Information Overload," *Computer Bits* 8, no. 3 (February 1998).
2. Ellen Goodman, "The Great American Spam Attack," *Washington Post,* February 9, 2002, p. A27.
3. Paul Krill, "Overcoming Information Overload," *InfoWorld* (www.infoworld.com), January 7, 2000.
4. Charles Jonscher, *The Evolution of Wired Life* (New York: Wiley, 1999), 36.
5. Jonscher, *Evolution,* 37.
6. David Schenk, *Data Smog* (San Francisco: HarperEdge, 1997), 37–38.
7. Peter Drucker, "The Icon Speaks: An Interview with Peter Drucker," *Information Outlook* 6, no. 2 (February 2002): 7–11.
8. Steven Collins, *Selfless Persons* (New York: Cambridge University Press), 1982.
9. "Press Zero to Disconnect," *Chicago Tribune,* March 2, 2002.
10. See, for example, *The Psychology of Meditation,* ed. Michael A. West (Oxford: Clarendon, 1987).
11. Drucker, "Icon Speaks," 8.

11 Seeking Harmony and Balance

*The fact that [Tiger] Woods acquired his religion of quiet in
contest-thrusting, commercial America is suggestive. "It helps
that my Buddhist upbringing has taught me to think of others
beyond myself and, frankly, I like Asian culture better than ours,"
he once said. "It's based on respect, discipline and personal
responsibility, and it's how my mother raised me."*[1]

PERHAPS THE CONNECTION BETWEEN BUDDHISM, GOLF, AND LIFE AS A LIBRARIAN MAY
seem somewhat far-fetched, but here is a picture of the superstar golfer drawing
on his mother's value system to achieve quiet and harmony in the face of pressures that bear a considerable resemblance to those felt by librarians and
libraries in a commercial, selfish world. Like Tiger Woods, we believe in excellence, respect, discipline, and thinking of others beyond ourselves. We believe
in the common good—a belief at great variance with much of the dominant
social and political thinking in today's America. We believe in values that
comfort the powerless and defend minorities in a world where the profit motive
reigns virtually unchallenged. We stand for selfless service, equal access, and in-
clusiveness in a world of egos, exclusion, and division.

The previous chapter contains a number of tactics for overcoming information overload and describes the many pressures that current circumstances
impose on those of us who work in libraries. These tactics, intended to make
working life easier from day to day, are responses to those circumstances and

concomitant stresses. However, if we are to have truly happy, productive, ful-filling lives, we need to go beyond tactical thinking to a way of looking at the world that will bring harmony and balance in library life and the rest of life. In short, we need a philosophy and an ethic of librarianship that incorporate our values (see chapter 6) and are the basis for resolving the dilemmas faced by us.

OUR RIGHT LIVELIHOOD

I have been thinking about a comprehensive ethic of librarianship for some time and, to that end, have read as widely as I can in philosophical, ethical, religious, and humanist texts to try to relate them to the practice of our profession. Some-what surprisingly for someone whose personal beliefs tend to the humanistic and the secular, this search has led me to the conclusion that the path to that particular understanding could do worse than begin with some central precepts of Buddhism applied in a purely secular environment and informed by the thinking of many philosophers and religious writers. The fourth Noble Truth of Buddhism tells us that there is a path to the cessation of suffering and the achievement of nirvana.[2] The ethics that bolster this truth are called the Eight-fold Path.[3] The eight parts of the Buddhist ethic are:

Right view or understanding: the holding of ethically correct views and taking responsibility for one's actions

Right-directed thoughts: that is, away from ill will and toward compassion and human kindness

Right speech: that is, abstaining from negative speech and writing

Right action: acting positively and with regard for others

Right livelihood: engaging in work that is of benefit to humankind

Right effort: that is, developing positive ways of thinking

Proper mindfulness: a keen awareness of the world and one's interior life

Right concentration or unification: meditation

These virtues, which are supposed to pervade the intellectual and social life of all, are intended to enable the follower of the way to achieve the four great qualities:

- Clarity
- Selflessness
- Universal friendliness
- Compassion

Surely we, whether adherents of a religion or of no religion, in search of nirvana or merely of a good way of living, could agree that it is reasonable to apply these ethics and virtues to librarianship? Can we not imagine a life as a librarian governed by the ethics and qualities put forward by the great teacher Gautama Buddha and found in one form or another in all the religions and humanist philosophies of the world? In the spirit of inquiry and leaving aside the rituals and stories that religions tell, there are lessons in each of them that can be of benefit to believers and nonbelievers alike. If one examines the writings of ethical humanists, who prefer reason to authority and revelation, one finds ways of living and universal qualities that bear a remarkable similarity to the Noble Truths and Eightfold Path of Buddhism and to the Golden Rule of Christianity—"do as you would be done by."[4] For example, the humanist Paul Kurtz writes:

> Presumably, at the higher reaches of ethics, one attempts to develop some impartiality in one's conduct and some appreciation of the "ethical point of view" and of decent ethical conduct in regard to others. The Golden Rule is deeply etched in sensible conduct.[5]

Or, in the communitarian Amitai Etzioni's words:

> The old golden rule (actually *rules,* because this precept appears in many cultures, albeit in somewhat different versions) contains an unspoken tension between what the ego would prefer to do to others and that which the golden rule urges ego to recognize as the right course of action.[6]

Buddhist ethics and virtues are based on precepts that are remarkably like the Golden Rule, thus subordinating the demands of the individual to the right courses of thought, speech, and action. For example, Buddhists are vegetarians because their beliefs in universal friendliness and compassion lead to a prohibition against eating fellow creatures—a good example of doing (or in this case, not doing) as one would wish to be (not) done by.

Would not all libraries be improved if run on the virtues of clarity, selflessness, friendliness, and compassion? Would not all librarians be happier and more effective if they all followed the Eightfold Path and the Golden Rule in their professional and private lives? This chapter explores the implications of these questions and proposes a philosophy and ethic of librarianship that are inspired by universal truths from the religions and value systems of humankind.

When Buddha considered the state of religion in his time, he rejected the current extremes (philosophical hair-splitting on the one hand and asceticism and withdrawal on the other) and formulated the Middle Way. The theological and philosophical wranglers of the fifth century B.C. were the forerunners of the extreme technophiles in libraries today—convinced of the truth and triumph of technology but differing violently on the exact means to technonirvana. The ascetics of that time can be compared to the rejecters of technology today—those who believe that a book, any book, is always preferable to an electronic resource. We must and should devise our own Middle Way in our "right livelihood" and achieve a balance in library collections and services that best serves our users and the mission of the library. In order to do this we must know, observe, and use ethical standards that embody our core values.

OUR CODE OF ETHICS

Though many librarians seem unaware of it, our professional association formulated a statement of ethical standards many decades ago and has restated and updated it periodically. The latest iteration of the American Library Association's Code of Ethics was adopted in June 1995.[7] It states:

I. We provide the highest level of service to all library users through appropriate and usefully organized resources; equitable service policies; equitable access; and accurate, unbiased, and courteous responses to all requests.

II. We uphold the principles of intellectual freedom and resist all efforts to censor library resources.

III. We protect each library user's right to privacy and confidentiality with respect to information sought or received and resources consulted, borrowed, acquired or transmitted.

IV. We recognize and respect intellectual property rights.

V. We treat co-workers and other colleagues with respect, fairness and good faith, and advocate conditions of employment that safeguard the rights and welfare of all employees of our institutions.

VI. We do not advance private interests at the expense of library users, colleagues, or our employing institutions.

VII. We distinguish between our personal convictions and professional duties and do not allow our personal beliefs to interfere with fair representation of the aims of our institutions or the provision of access to their information resources.

VIII. We strive for excellence in the profession by maintaining and enhancing our own knowledge and skills, by encouraging the professional development of co-workers, and by fostering the aspirations of potential members of the profession.

The reader will note the coincidence of the number of statements in the Code of Ethics and the Buddhist Eightfold Path. Less superficially, there is a remarkable overlap in the abstract ethic of the Eightfold Path and its concomitant four great qualities on the one hand, and the profession-specific and detailed statements of the ALA Code on the other. There can be no doubt that librarianship is a manifestation of having a "right livelihood"—one based on values, service, and selflessness; one that seeks to help others and avoid harm to others; one that aspires to the qualities of clarity, compassion, universal friendliness, and selflessness. More specifically, one can discern the application of the ethic and virtues of Buddhism in each of the eight stipulations of the Code:

I. The reference in the Code to the various aspects of service, equity of access, and treating people well and fairly recall the Buddhist virtues of right thought, right action, and right-directed thoughts.

II. Upholding intellectual freedom and resisting censorship are manifestations of right views, right-directed thoughts, and right mindfulness.

III. The Code tells us to protect the privacy of the library user and his or her confidentiality. We do this out of universal friendliness and right-directed thoughts leading to the right actions we take to protect privacy.

IV. Intellectual property rights (which are under serious attack commercially and philosophically because of some aspects of technology) arise because society respects the right of creators to own the fruits of their labor. In recognizing those rights, we are extending the hand of human friendliness and thinking and acting ethically.

V. Everything in the Eightfold Path and the great qualities of selflessness and compassion tell us to treat our colleagues with respect and good faith and to strive for positive and humane working conditions in our libraries.

VI. "We do not advance private interests at the expense of library users, colleagues, or employing institutions" because of our belief in right thoughts, actions, and effort—virtues informed by selflessness.

VII. The Code enjoins us not to confuse our personal ideas and beliefs with our professional duties. This instruction calls on us to make a right effort and exercise selflessness in an area where deep personal beliefs may come into play. Neither the Code nor the Eightfold Path are always easy to follow in such instances.

VIII. The search for excellence in our profession through self-development, helping others to develop, and supporting all professional aspirations is another manifestation of right action, right effort, selflessness, and compassion.

THE COMMON GOOD

Amitai Etzioni is another seeker of a middle way. In his book *The New Golden Rule,* he advances a theory called "communitarianism," which envisages a society that balances freedom and order, tradition and modernity, and self and community.[8] This passage from his book is of particular relevance to our topic:

> The communitarian quest, as I see it, is to seek a way to blend elements of tradition (order based on virtues) with elements of modernity (well protected autonomy). This, in turn, entails finding an equilibrium between universal individual rights and the common good (too often viewed as incompatible concepts), between self and community, and, above all, how such an equilibrium can be achieved and sustained.[9]

The age-old conflict between the desires of the individual and the necessities of an ordered society presents us with an insoluble dilemma. Instead of a solution in favor of one or the other (which can only result in anarchy or the world of *1984*), humans and the societies in which they live have learned to accept an imperfect admixture in which the balance is tipped one way or the other to a greater or lesser extent. The differences between today's United States, China, and, say, Sweden are delineated by the nature of the balance between individualism and order in their social systems. My point is that none of the three is tilted decisively toward anarchy or Orwell's nightmare, though aspects of their societies may have tendencies toward either.

Libraries, which are quintessential manifestations of the common good, have always favored order and society over individualism. Individualistic shelving arrangements, classification schemes, instruction programs, and collection development have never found favor with those who run libraries, work in libraries, and use libraries. An individualistic cataloguer is an oxymoron, though now I come to think of it . . . but I digress! We prize order and orderly behavior, having learned over the years that both pay dividends in the form of effective and efficient service. There is little wonder in the fact that it has been difficult to integrate the utter anarchism of the Internet into our programs and services. Difficult, but, as many libraries have shown, not impossible. It should be noted, however, that the many successes libraries have achieved have always been based on the imposition of some kind of order, some kind of restraint of the more freewheeling aspects of digital communication. The paradox is that although we prize and use order to render our service to society, we render that service one individual at a time, with the ultimate aim of providing the ultimate freedom—the freedom of the individual to read, study, and absorb anything that he or she wishes. We use order to set minds free, to allow each human being to expand his or her mind, to learn, and to understand. A human being who understands the world and has access to all the world's information and recorded knowledge knows real freedom, no matter what kind of society he or she lives in. An individual deprived of the whole range of library service is as mentally enslaved as an individual deprived of political or economic freedom is physically enslaved. That is why we librarians should never tire of our work toward and for the common good.

If we are to work for the common good, we must have a clear idea of what it is and from whence it arises. In particular, we need to know which values we share (as librarians and in society as a whole), because shared values are a necessary precondition of the concept of a common good. To take just one example among many, let us consider the values of academic librarians and the common good to which they are dedicated. Like all of us, academic librarians live in several worlds—in this case the worlds of a particular library, a particular profession, a particular academic institution, a particular urban or rural community, state, region, and nation. It is difficult enough to perceive shared values and formulate a common good in the smaller of these concentric and overlapping circles—how much more difficult it must be in the case of the larger (our profession and nation). Fortunately, apart from now-discredited right-wing leaders, most notoriously Margaret Thatcher (who claimed "There is no such thing as society"), there seems to be a broad (if shallow) consensus across mainstream political parties, religions, and social thinkers that some wider or narrower concept of the common good is a vital part of social life.[10] It is rare today to find any politician, educator, or businessperson who actively and openly opposes libraries, and in most cases, our problems are caused more by indifference than overt hostility. Within our profession, and especially within our own institution, we find a rooted belief in the value of libraries—one that is almost taken for granted. There may be arguments within librarianship or within a particular library as to how we best exercise our pursuit of the common good, but there is little argument about the value of libraries per se.

In the wider circles of the town, state, and region in which the library is situated, that easy assumption may well be questioned. Look at what happened in California in the wake of the great tax revolt of the late 1970s. Cash-strapped municipalities and counties cut their library services to the bone; and cash-starved schools depleted and, in many cases, deleted their libraries along with other "peripheral" programs such as art, band, etc. Nearly a quarter century later, those services have not recovered from being perceived as, at best, peripheral to the common good. You can be sure that the librarians who lost their school library jobs, the branch librarians in closed library branches, and the former users of the closed branches (especially the old and the young) had a very clear idea of the common good that was denied them. You can also be sure that they were right. Had all those public library branches (and, in a few cases, whole systems) not been closed and had California's public schools not degraded or lost their fine school libraries, we would not be lamenting the low reading and writing skills of university graduates in that state today. Cause and effect operates in the nonprofit areas of society as much as in the profit-based sector.

BALANCE AND CLARITY

Just as the common good in society demands equilibrium between individualism and order—between the demands of the self and the good of all—the practice of librarianship demands equilibrium between tradition and innovation, the old and the new, the needs of the many and the needs of minorities or individuals. The task is to use the three lanterns of our values (service, intellectual freedom, equity of access), our code of ethics, and the Eightfold Path and concomitant virtues to light our way as we wrestle with the issues, dilemmas, and problems of the age in which we live and work. In negotiating these issues, we must always seek harmony, balance, and the middle way. The following are some areas in which the search for equilibrium is most important:

- Collections: electronic resources and "traditional" resources
- Establishing priorities in the allocation of resources to various library activities, services, and programs
- Serving the common good and meeting the needs of the individual
- Bridging the library divide

- Making progress through collaboration and cooperation
- Balancing the demands of library working life with the other areas of life
- Preserving the human record

I have already discussed the nature of modern collections in previous chapters and how they must reach out to encompass not only remote electronic resources, but also those materials held by other libraries that are readily available through library cooperation made feasible by technology. Right thought, right action, and universal friendliness lead us to participate in such resource-sharing and other cooperative schemes in a fair and moral manner—that is, by playing our full part and not exploiting the situation by contributing less than we derive. Taking the latter path is not only unethical but also, as so often in life, impractical and counterproductive. All collaborations ultimately depend on good faith and mutuality of interest buttressed by a sincere wish to play one's part. Each party balances its needs against its capability to contribute, and the ethical thing to do is also the practically beneficial thing to do.

There is also the question of balance between expenditures on electronic materials and those on print and other tangible materials. In this area, right thought is that which is not influenced by fads and societal pressures but which instead sees the situation clearly, recognizing the strengths, weaknesses, and value of each form of communication. Once this clarity of thought is achieved, all falls into place and one is able to set priorities and make resource allocations for different kinds of library material in a balanced and productive manner.

Another resource allocation issue lies in the question of equitable and balanced funding for different programs, departments, and services within the library. Here again balance and clarity are all. As we all know, libraries are chronically underfunded, which makes it even more important that such funds as we have are distributed efficiently and fairly. One particular area in which many library administrators have not demonstrated mindfulness, right thought, or right action is that of the balance between public services (chiefly reference and instruction) and technical processing (cataloguing, acquisitions, etc.). Libraries that used to have large and productive acquisitions and cataloguing departments have downgraded and degraded those services to the point at which they have become deprofessionalized, demoralized, and unproductive. Forty or more years ago, such departments were wasteful of professional resources in that they often assigned clerical and quasi-professional work to librarians. The OCLC in particular, and other aspects of library automation in general, pointed up the folly of that approach, making it possible to shrink the size of technical processing departments and concentrate professional work in professional hands.

These should all have been positive developments but, as it turns out, have often been negative. Many administrators have treated technical processing, particularly cataloguing and the professional quotient of acquisitions work, as an irrelevant drain on the library's purse. There is an academic library in California in which *every* employee with an M.L.S. degree works in the reference/instruction department. In such a library, acquisitions is treated as a purely clerical operation that is at the mercy of the library's vendors; and original cataloguing is not done, or done by library assistants, or sold off to outsourcers and other commercial services. Not only has such a library lost a great deal of expertise (one does not envy them when next acquiring and installing an online system without cataloguing expertise to sustain them), but it has also fatally wounded its collection development program, degraded its catalogue, and failed to play its part in collaborative enterprises by failing to add high-quality catalogue records to the joint database. Such misguided priorities cannot be viewed as ethical. All users of the library are entitled to a budgetary and financial structure that funds the programs and services they need, and that maintains the pillars of the library (its bibliographic architecture and public services) equally.

We have seen that the tension between the needs and wants of the individual and the needs of society lies at the heart of our ethical considerations. Libraries are creations of society and are sustained by society, but they are there for individuals and for minorities as small as one. Here again, we need ethical lamps to ensure that we can find a balance. Look, for example, at the idea that collections in small libraries and those in small communities should be governed by "community standards"—a doctrine that has led to the many sad absurdities chronicled in the ALA's annual list of challenged and banned books. A public library in a small town is there to serve the inhabitants of that town, but should its collection development policy be based on the opinions of the majority (as divined in their "community standards") and thus prevent a teenaged library user from reading *The Catcher in the Rye?* In short, we are for the common good but do not take a majoritarian or even utilitarian point of view. The common good is the good of each individual in a community funded collectively, not the good of those in the community who think alike. Ultimately, the belief that the common good is advanced by the freedom of the individual restricted only by adherence to the Golden Rule is at the heart of library ethics. In particular, the freedom of the individual to read, write, and think whatever he or she wishes is a central issue. Will that always lead to right thought and right speech in all cases? Of course not, but it is the task of the individual to try to achieve right thought on his or her own—it cannot be imposed. The ethical path leads always to the defense of freedom of thought, reading, and expression, but it is a path that is difficult to follow in some situations, especially in the case of small and unpopular minorities.

The ethics of the library divide are quite clear and should in theory present few dilemmas to any librarian. Collectively and individually, we deplore the inequities in the provision of library services that mirror the deep inequities in the wider society. We would, if we could, remove them so that the very poor had access to library services every bit as good as those enjoyed by the affluent, and every child and old person had a well-stocked, well-staffed, technologically advanced library close at hand. However, we have to deal with the world as it is—a world not devoted to the ideals of universal friendliness and the common good, but one that accepts and even, in some cases, welcomes inequities and differences in matters great and small. The ethical quandary that faces each librarian devoted to equity of library service is the degree to which he or she should work in the wider societal and political context to bring about changes that will narrow the library divide. In doing so, one is taking a decided stance in the eternal battle between tradition and progress on the side of the latter. At that point, the best thing one can be called is "progressive," with other, harsher words just around the corner. The librarians who established free public libraries in the late nineteenth and early twentieth centuries were regarded, quite correctly, as on the side of social change and opposed to the side of reaction. Librarians today who argue for a more equitable dispersion of resources in society—knowing that it is the only way to narrow the library divide—will also be regarded as being "on the left," which of course they are, if being "on the right" means being in favor of preserving the existing order. The existing order includes the library divide and all the other inequities in society. Those who want to change that order, out of compassion, clarity, and right thought are, of necessity, on the side of change and progress. It is no coincidence that librarians, in this respect, are very similar to those who labor in similar vineyards—teaching, social work, nursing, etc. Temperamentally, most librarians are not inclined to revolutionary change (probably because of the order and stability that most libraries and library services require), but in this case they have had to choose sides, even if only to stand on the moderate side of the progressive wing.

Libraries have always cooperated when they could, but that cooperation was limited for many years by practicalities of the technology of the day. There were union card catalogues, but the problems of maintaining them and the impossibility of keeping them current made them fallible instruments of library cooperation. Cooperative (as opposed to centralized) cataloguing was very difficult in the pre-automation era. The lack of modern communications technology tended to isolate libraries in many ways. All this started to change rapidly in the age of library automation and bibliographic standardization that began in the early 1970s. Libraries could contribute to and use shared databases that were completely current and, since they were based on commonly agreed standards (MARC, *AACR2*, etc.), reasonably coherent. At a later stage, the catalogues of other libraries, even those not participating in one's own shared database, became available. The crowning achievement was the OCLC database—the nearest thing to a universal bibliography the world has ever seen—linked to a global resource-sharing system. All these schemes worked and still work because libraries participated in them in an ethical manner and in the spirit of universal friendliness.

Another set of ethical issues is posed by libraries of different kinds collaborating on projects in the same locality. Each library is funded differently and has a different mission. The balance sought is one that weighs the needs of the population the library is funded to serve and the needs of the users of the other libraries involved in the collaborative project. The interests of the two are not necessarily antithetical and good projects are those in which everyone benefits, but ethical dilemmas do arise when the interests of one group clash with the interests of another.

Librarians, like the members of any other profession, live in several worlds simultaneously. Though in many ways we have lost the sense of mission and a higher calling that is found in writings from Melvil Dewey to Lawrence Clark Powell, most of us have some sense of vocation—an ethic of service to individuals and our community and to the high ideals of learning—that leaches out from our working life into our other lives. Just as a doctor is a doctor when not practicing medicine, the typical librarian is a librarian in most of her waking hours. The incurable itch to inform, to make orderly, to communicate our love of reading and knowledge, is still present in many of us, even when we are not actually pursuing our livelihood. This used to be entirely a bookish profession. It is less so now, but most of us know (or are) a librarian whose hobby, often carried out with the help of computers, employs many of our library skills and interests. I have known librarians who are gourmet cooks with beautifully organized databases of recipes retrievable by any combination of variables. There are librarians who have created web pages devoted to the Rolling Stones, the tarot, or Indonesian politics that are marvels of organization and retrievability. Happy is the club whose secretary is a librarian—you can be sure that its records are detailed and organized and its archives scrupulously maintained. The balance we seek is not that of sealed and compartmentalized aspects of our lives but one in which work life, family life, and our other lives each inform the other and all are infused with right thought, speech, and action.

We have an ethical imperative to extend our universal friendliness and right action to future generations by carrying out our unique responsibility to preserve the human record and transmit it to future generations. Our Code of Ethics tells us that we have a responsibility to serve all library users, and what are collection development and cataloguing but actions taken on behalf of all future users of the library as well as those now living? Beyond these individual acts in individual libraries, we as a profession have a responsibility to the human record that transcends almost any other issue facing librarianship today. We cannot and must not shirk this duty, because to do so would be to fail ethically as well as in practical terms. Here again the watchwords are balance and harmony married to clarity of thought. There are many proposed paths to the preservation of the human record. We need to think about each of them and weigh the consequences of each.

ENVOI

As ever, these are interesting times and many librarians feel buffeted by change, alienated from one or another aspect of modern libraries, and challenged by the two-headed dragon of shrinking resources and technological demands. There is, I am convinced, only one way to restore our delight in our jobs and balance to our lives. It is to look at where we are and where we have been with clarity of vision and to act on the basis of the understanding that clarity brings. To understand the processes that are at work and the forces that shape our working lives is to take control of both. Having done so, we can all aspire to work in a library that matches the ideal described by Lawrence Clark Powell more than thirty years ago:

> Good hands have made it a place of orderly arrangement, of good housekeeping. Good heads have resulted in [materials in all formats] of intelligent choice, their contents absorbed by the staff. Good hearts have made it a warm and welcoming place.[11]

NOTES

1. Simon Barnes, "Enter Woods, Muirfield's Mystery Man," [London] *Times Online,* July 15, 2002.
2. Nirvana may be defined as "a timeless imperturbable state beyond change and suffering" (Peter Harvey, "Buddhist Visions of the Human Predicament and Its Resolution," in *Buddhism,* ed. Peter Harvey [New York: Continuum, 2001], 63).

3. Harvey, *Buddhism,* 88–90.

4. "Do unto others as you would have them do unto you" (Matthew 7:12).

5. Paul Kurtz, *Forbidden Fruit: The Ethics of Humanism* (Buffalo, N.Y.: Prometheus Books, 1988), 169.

6. Amitai Etzioni, *The New Golden Rule: Community and Morality in a Democratic Society* (New York: BasicBooks, 1996), xviii.

7. ALA Code of Ethics, available at http://www.ala.org/alaorg/oif/ethics.html.

8. Etzioni, *New Golden Rule.*

9. Ibid., xviii.

10. "And there is no such thing as society. There are individual men and women and there are families." (Margaret Thatcher in an interview entitled "Aids, Education and the Year 2000," *Woman's Own,* October 3, 1987, pp. 8–10.)

11. Lawrence Clark Powell, *The Three Hs* (Los Angeles: Press in the Gatehouse, 1971). I trust Dr. Powell's shade will forgive me the substitution for "books and periodicals."

INDEX

A

AACR2
electronic resources, 90
history, 84
realia in, 55
and universal bibliographic control, 85–86
academic libraries
buildings for, 6
and literacy, 50
need for, 4
values of, 140
access, equity of, 37, 77–78
"access not ownership" concept, 67
accuracy of information. *See* Authenticity
acquisitions, 142–43
advertising, 96, 123
aliteracy
definition, 41
as enemy of learning, 76
research into, 117
American Library Association
Code of Ethics, 137–39
conferences on professional education, 10, 119–21
Office for Literacy and Outreach Services, 44–46
Paris Exposition of 1900, 24
analogies, 47
Anglo-American Cataloguing Rules, Second Edition. See AACR2
appointments for reference service, 70, 71
archives, digitized, 64
Arion Press, xii–xiii

Aristophanes of Byzantium, 72
Arms, William Y., 28–32
articles in journals
as first thoughts, 132–33
and publishing technology, 63
assessment. *See* Evaluation
audiovisual materials, cataloguing of, 87
authenticity
electronic resources, 87
importance of, 99
printed books, 73
authority of information. *See* Authenticity

B

Babbage, Charles, 22
baby boomers, 9
Baker, Nicholson, 12–13
balance of library roles, 5, 141–46
benevolence, decreased, 124
Berliner, Emile, 21
Bible, textual authenticity of, 99–100
bibliographic control. *See also*
Categorization of Web
and education in cataloguing, 120
and preservation of knowledge, 112
for print materials, 82–86
of Web, 114–15
Bloom, Harold, 42
books, printed
and civilization, 48
as complete ideas, 133
current trends, 33–34
stability and authenticity of, 73
tactility of, 46

breaks from work, 127–28
Briet, Suzanne, 55
Buddhism, 135–37
budgeting, priorities in, 32–33, 35, 98, 142
burnout. *See* Despair
Bush, Vannevar, 11

C

California Council of the Humanities, 50
Callimachus of Cyrene, 72
cardiovascular stress, 124
Carnegie Endowment for International Peace, 17
Carroll, Lewis, 65n5
catalogues
    printed, 8
    vs. search engines, 29
    web-based, 12
cataloguing, 82–94
    and archives, 64
    and metadata, 114–15
categorization of Web, 60–65
cave paintings, 15–16
censorship
    and community standards, 143
    and value of web materials, 54
change, 14–15, 17
changeability. *See* Fixity; Malleability
Chicago literacy campaign, 50
children's librarians, 49, 127
circulation records, privacy of, 79
clarity and balance, 135, 141–46
collaboration. *See* Interlibrary cooperation
collection development and technical processing, 143. *See also* Selection of electronic resources
collections. *See* Content of collections; Library collections
colonization and technology, 19–20
commercial websites, 62
common good, 139–41
Commonwealth War Graves Commission, 64
communications technology
    challenges of, 95

fear of, 130
history, 14–26, 30–32
in libraries, 27–39
as revolutionary, 20, 22
communitarianism, 139
community standards and intellectual freedom, 143
compassion. *See also* Benevolence, decreased
    achieving, 135, 136
computer hackers, 105–6
computer screens, reading from, 107–8, 124
computer technology. *See* Technology
computer viruses, 106–7
confidentiality. *See* Privacy
confusion, 124
content of collections
    digitization of, 12
    vs. technology of messages, 7, 16
    vulnerability of, 18, 106
cooperation. *See* Interlibrary cooperation
cooperative cataloguing
    and bibliographic control, 83
    electronic resources, 92
    and technology, 145
Copernican principle
    and communications technology, 16–17
    defined, xiv
    in libraries, 2
core competences
    conference on, 10
    research in, 119–21
core values. *See* Values
costs of scholarly materials, 28
creative works, 64–65
critical thinking
    in library instruction, 103
    and literacy, 46
Crunden, F. M., 24
currency of materials, 74, 98
curriculum in library schools, 9–11, 120
    See also Library education
Cutter, Charles Ammi, 24, 71

D

data, 124

decision making, impaired, 124

democracy, education for, 79–80

despair, 124

digital divide, 36–39

    increased by technology, 105

    and library divide, 4, 119

    and other social inequities, 77–78

digital media

    and earlier technologies, 30–32

    of enduring value, 7

    proportion of collections, 33

digitization

    challenges of, 95, 97

    in libraries, 12

    and preservation, 13

"disintermediation." *See* Internet, myth that
    "everything is on it"

distance learning, 4. *See also* Remote users

diversity of libraries, 3–4

documents, definition of, 54–59

dot.coms, xii–xiii, 9

Drucker, Peter, 17, 128

Dublin Core, 90–92

E

e-books, 47, 98, 118, 119

e-commerce, 17

e-mail

    collection of, 108

    compulsion to check, 122–23, 127

    confidentiality of, 78

    vs. pen-and-ink letters, 16

e-mail reference, 70, 78

Eastman, George, 20

economic impact of computer technology,
    98

Edison, Thomas, 21

Eightfold Path

    and ALA Code of Ethics, 138–39

    Buddhist teaching, 135–37

electronic discussion lists, 126

electronic journals

    costs of, 115–16

    current trends, 35

    and publishing practice, 63–64

electronic resources

    budgeting for, 35–36

    cataloguing of, 86–88

    and equity of access, 78

    in library collections, 8

    selection of, 88–89

    similarity to print resources, 67, 90

    static or cumulative, 114

    vs. websites, 113–14

Eliot, George, ix

elitism, 50

English language, dominance of, 105

entertainment and recreations

    in 1901, 23

    and quality of reading matter, 42

ephemera, 60–62. *See also* Superficiality of
    electronic resources

equipment for electronic resources, 35, 67

escapist literature, 133

ethical humanism and the Noble Truths,
    136

ethics of librarianship

    ALA Code of Ethics, 137–39

    and balance of individual and commu-
        nity needs, 143

    and Eightfold Path, 135

Etzioni, Amitai, 136, 139

evaluation in reference service, 75

evolution of libraries, 3

exclusivity, 103–5. *See also* Access, equity
    of

expert systems, 70

F

family life, 131

Fessenden, Reginald, 22

film as creative medium, 64

filtering, 54

finding aids, 64

fixity

    of electronic resources, 87

    of printed materials, 100

food in libraries, 7

forgeries, 100

fragility of electronic documents, 98
Fresno County (Calif.), 37–38, 111
Fretwell, John, 25
friendliness, universal, 135, 136
Friese-Greene, William, 21
frustration, 124

G

Gandhi, Mohandas, 103–4
Gates Foundation, 4
genealogists, 64
globalization and Web, 52
Golden Rule and the Noble Truths, 136
Google, 29–30, 60–62, 98
Gorman, Michael (author), 100
Gorman, Michael (musician), 101–2
The Grapes of Wrath (Steinbeck), 50
great books approach, 50
Green, Samuel S., 68–69

H

hardware, 35, 67
harmony and balance, 134–47
hobbies, 131
Huse, H. R., 43

I

IFLA International Meeting of Cataloguing
    Experts (IMCE), 84, 85
illiteracy, 76. *See also* Aliteracy; Literacy
indexing in specific disciplines, 29–30
individual and society
    balancing needs of, 139, 141
    and funding, 143–44
informal discussion, 130
information
    definitions, 111
    processing of, 123–24
"information centers," 5, 7
information overload, 122–24
information revolution
    arguments for, 30–32
    as evolutionary, 16–18
information science, 111–12

information sources other than libraries,
    61–62
infrastructure for electronic resources, 35
Institute of Museum and Library Services, 9
intellectual freedom
    in ALA Code of Ethics, 137
    and community standards, 143
    and Eightfold Path, 138
    and reference work, 73–74
    and value of web materials, 54
intellectual property
    in ALA Code of Ethics, 137
    and Eightfold Path, 138
    and technology, 118
interlibrary cooperation
    and balance of users' needs, 145
    and Eightfold Path, 142
    and technology, 144
interlibrary loan, 8, 66
International Meeting of Cataloguing
    Experts (IMCE), 84, 85
Internet. *See also* Web
    anarchism of, 140
    cooperative cataloguing, 92
    evaluation of, 74
    myth that "everything is on it," 27–28,
        71
    need for analysis of, 89
    and poor people, 37–39
    as source of free materials, 28
inventions, effects of, 19–20
invisible Web, 52
ISBD (International Standard Bibliographic
    Description), 83, 84, 85, 90

J

Japanese American Network website,
    56–58
Jewett, Charles Coffin, 83
joy of reading, 45
Joyce, James, 99–100
judgment, impaired, 124

K

knowledge
    computer retrieval of, 107

as concern of librarians, 111
history and preservation of, 18–19
in library instruction programs, 103
in printed texts, 47
processing of, 124
and sustained reading, 49
vs. information, 23
Kurtz, Paul, 136

L

learning process, research into, 117–18
Lee, Harper, 50
letters, pen-and-ink, 16, 20
librarians
changes in, 8–11
education for reference, 120
ethic of, 28, 135, 145
interaction with users, 68–69
and promotion of literary, 46
and rationalism, 74
role of, 29, 49–51, 73
vs. information scientists, 111
librarianship as learned profession, 47
library automation
contributing to stress, 125
and funding for technical processing,
142–43
history, 12
and interlibrary resource sharing, 66
vulnerability of, 106
library buildings, 4–7, 25
library catalogues. *See* Catalogues
library collections. *See also* Content of collections
balance between electronic and nonelectronic resources, 141, 142
and commercial information, 62
and ephemera, 61
as essential services, 7
expansion of definition, 8
history, 66–67
as preservers of knowledge, 18
library divide
bridging of, 141
and digital divide, 4, 119
and wider societal problems, 37, 144

library education
curriculum, 9–11, 120
for reference work, 72
research in, 110, 119–21
library instruction programs, 103
Library Journal, technology in, 24–26
Library of Congress
in 1901, 25
American Memory Project, 53, 64
America's Story website, 7
"Bibliographic Control of Web
Resources," 92
catalogue card service, 83–84
library schools. *See* Library education
library services
in ALA Code of Ethics, 137
and digital divide, 119
and Eightfold Path, 138
library systems department, 36
Licklider, J. C. R., 11–12
life, getting a, 128, 142
life of the mind, 125
lifelong learning
and civilization, 48
and literacy, 47, 117
and reference librarians, 76–77
literacy
in 1901, 23
and civilization, 48
definitions of, 40–41
effect of technology on, 20
as essential to success, 43
forces against, 44
promotion of, 46
and reference services, 76–77
research in, 116–18
literacy, functional or technical. *See*
Aliteracy
literacy campaigns, 50
Lubetzky, Seymour, 86

M

magazines, readership of, 20
malleability, 99–102
management, fads in, 130–31, 132

manuscripts, hand-copied
   mutability of, 100–101
   preservation of, 112
MARC record
   and bibliographic control, 83, 84–85
   and Dublin Core, 90
   influence on technology adoption, 12
Matthews, Gordon, 129
Mayan bark-cloth, 71
meaning of life, 23
Means, Russell, 104
medical information, currency of, 74
meditation, 132
meetings, coping with, 126–27
metadata, 89–90, 91, 114–15
microfilms, 19, 21
Middle Way, 136–37
Middlemarch (Eliot), ix
minority users, 143
mutability
   of electronic documents, 87, 98
   as positive attribute, 104–5
   preservation considerations, 114

N

Napster, 118
A Nation Online, 37
National Academy Press, 118
National Union Catalog, 83–84
natural language interfaces, 115
newsgroups, 126
newspapers, readership of, 20
nineteenth century, innovations in, 22
"no," saying, 129
nonprint media
   distribution of, 118
   trends, 34–35

O

objects as documents, 55
OCLC
   Dublin Core, 90–92
   as technology, 12
   as union catalogue, 8
O'Donnell, James J., 47

oral tradition, 49, 104
order in library service, 140, 145
organization of collections
   electronic resources, 87
   and reference librarians, 72
overconfidence, 124

P

Paris Principles, 86
parish registers, 64
peer pressure, 131–32
personal web pages, 61
perspective. *See* Vision, wider
phonograph, invention of, 21
photocopying technology, 25
photography
   effect of technology on, 20
   in 19th-century libraries, 24–25
plagiarism, 100
political action and library divide, 144
poor people. *See also* Digital divide; Library
   divide
   and communications technology, 105
   and the Internet, 37–39
pornography, 62
Powell, Lawrence Clark, 46–47, 146
precision and recall, 102, 109n6
preservation
   and definition of document, 58
   of digital information, 7, 18, 93, 98
   as ethic of librarianship, 146
   problem of, 12–13
   and reference services, 70–71
   research on, 112–14
Print Age, preservation in, 112
print-derived resources on Web, 62–63
printed books. *See* Books, printed
printing, effect of technology on, 21
priorities
   allocation of resources, 141, 142
   in budgeting, 32–33, 35
   setting, 127, 131
privacy
   in ALA Code of Ethics, 137
   and avoiding overload, 129–30

and Eightfold Path, 138
and reference work, 78–79
private interests in ALA Code of Ethics, 137, 138
professional values. *See* Values
programs, public
in academic libraries, 50
promoting reading, 49
The Protocols of the Elders of Zion, 54, 65n2
provenance and authenticity of texts, 100
public services
balance with technical services in funding, 142
stereotypes of, 67–68
publishers and publishing
authenticity of, 74
and computer technology, 118–19
and preservation, 113
pulp magazines, 44

Q

quality of information. *See also* Authenticity
metadata, 90, 91
on Web, 53

R

radio
as information revolution, 107
invention of, 22
rationalism, 74–76
reading, sustained
and full literacy, 41, 49
personal, 132–33
vs. information literacy, 45, 46
reading and literacy, 40–51
reading competitions, 49
reading process, 43
real job, concentration on, 130–31
realia, cataloguing of, 55
recall and precision, 102, 109n6
recreations. *See* Entertainment and recreations
recruitment, 9
reference interview, 68–69, 75
reference questions, classification of, 75

reference services, 66–81
and definition of document, 58
related works, web links as, 59
remote users, 78. *See also* Distance learning
research
need for, 110–21
suitability of Web for, 12
resignation, 124
retrievability of electronic resources, 87
right livelihood, 135–37, 138
Rodriguez, Richard, 43
role of the library, 5, 141–46. *See also* Librarians, role of
Roosevelt, Eleanor, 42
Rutenbeck, Jeff, 97

S

Schenk, David, 124
scholarly communication, research in, 115–16
scholarly materials
availability on Web, 28
stability and authenticity of, 73–74
scholarly publishing
changes in serials publishing, 116
and electronic journals, 63
school libraries, 49
search engines
drawbacks of, 98, 102
in library instruction, 103
vs. library catalogues, 29
Seattle literacy campaign, 50
selection of electronic resources, 54, 70–71, 75, 88–89
selectivity, 102–3
self-development in ALA Code of Ethics, 138, 139
self-sacrifice, avoiding, 128–29
selflessness
dangers of, 128–29
in Eightfold Path, 135, 138
"sensitive" topics
and privacy, 79
and reference services, 73
serials. *See also* Electronic journals
costs of, 115
current trends, 34–35

series, cataloguing of, 58–59
service ethic of librarians, 28, 72–73
shelving systems, 25
shopping mall libraries, 7
social change and activism, 144
sound, effect of technology on, 21
sound recordings, 35
spam, 123
SPARC (Scholarly Publishing and
    Academic Resources Coalition), 63
special libraries, 50
standards. *See also* Bibliographic control
    for cataloguing, 83
    and interlibrary cooperation, 145
    metadata, 91
Steinbeck, John, 50
stewardship and reference work, 70–72
storytelling, 49
stress, 122–33
superficiality of electronic resources,
    107–8. *See also* Ephemera
Swinton, Campbell, 22

T

taxonomy for web materials
    and criteria for preservation, 113–14
    and mutability, 60
team management, 130
technical services
    balance with public services in funding,
        142
    stereotypes of, 67–68
technology
    challenges of, 97
    effects of, 19–24
    and equity of access, 78
    in libraries, 3, 11–12, 24–26
    stages of, xi
    vs. content, 16
telephones
    history, 21
    and remote users, 78
television, 22, 64–65
Third World
    digital divide, 37
    technological exploitation of, 20

To Kill a Mockingbird (Lee), 50
tolerance and value of web materials, 54
traditional library services, 98, 141
transformational time, theory of, 95
transportation inventions, 19
trends, 131–32
triage services, 70
trust. *See* Authenticity
twentieth century, life in, 23

U

Ulysses (Joyce), 99–100
universal bibliographic control. *See*
    Bibliographic control
universal friendliness, 135, 136
universities without libraries, 4

V

values
    ALA conference on, 119–21
    and balance, 141
    and common good, 140
    and reference service, 70–80
Van Winkle, William, 123
video recordings, 35
vision, wider, 127
vision problems. *See* Computer screens,
    reading from
visual stimulation, 20–21
vocabulary control
    and Dublin Core, 91
    and metadata, 115
    in specific disciplines, 29–30
vocation of librarians, 145
voice mail, 129

vulnerability of electronic resources, 105–7

W

Wales, J. Rufus, 24
Warren, Louis A., 44
Web, 52–65. *See also* Internet
    bibliographic control of, 114–15
    categorization of, 60–65

problems, 53–54
quality of information on, 12
web links, cataloguing of, 59
web pages
    collection of, 108
    as creative media, 64–65
    as documents, 56
web surfing, 131
websites
    vs. electronic documents, 113–14
Wells, H. G., 79–80

Western civilization, 48, 103–4
wisdom, 124
Woods, Tiger, 134
Woolf, Virginia, 45
work and family issues, 142,
    145
World Wide Web. *See* Web

Y

youth and library schools, 9

MICHAEL GORMAN is dean of library services at the Henry Madden Library, California State University, Fresno. From 1977 to 1988 he worked at the University of Illinois (Urbana) Library as, successively, director of technical services, director of general services, and acting university librarian. From 1966 to 1977 he was successively head of cataloguing at the *British National Bibliography*, a member of the British Library Planning Secretariat, and head of the Office of Bibliographic Standards in the British Library. He has taught at library schools in his native Britain and in the United States—most recently at the University of California, Los Angeles.

He was the first editor of the *Anglo-American Cataloguing Rules, Second Edition* (1978) and of the 1988 revision of that work. He is also the editor of *The Concise AACR2*, third edition (1999) and *Technical Services Today and Tomorrow*, second edition (1998). His book *Future Libraries: Dreams, Madness, and Reality* (1995), coauthored with Walt Crawford, was honored with the 1997 Blackwell's Scholarship Award. His most recent book, *Our Enduring Values* (2000), was the winner of the ALA's Highsmith Award in 2001 for the best book on librarianship. Gorman is the author of hundreds of articles in professional and scholarly journals. He has given numerous presentations at international, national, and state conferences.

Michael Gorman is a fellow of the (British) Library Association, the 1979 recipient of the Margaret Mann Citation, and the 1992 recipient of the Melvil Dewey Medal.

Printed in the United States
202620BV00003B/85-150/A

9 780838 908464